DISCARD

Special Events
From A to Z

*This handbook is dedicated to
the special people behind the scenes of school events
who make those events special for others.*

Special Events From A to Z

The Complete Educator's Handbook

Gayle Jasso

CORWIN PRESS, INC.
A Sage Publications Company
Thousand Oaks, California

For information address:

Corwin Press, Inc.
A Sage Publications Company
2455 Teller Road
Thousand Oaks, California 91320
E-mail: order@corwin.sagepub.com

SAGE Publications Ltd.
6 Bonhill Street
London EC2A 4PU
United Kingdom

SAGE Publications India Pvt. Ltd.
M-32 Market
Greater Kailash I
New Delhi 110 048 India

Printed in the United States of America

Library of Congress Cataloging-in-Publication Data

Jasso, Gayle.
    Special events from A to Z: The complete educator's handbook/
Gayle Jasso.
        p.   cm.
    ISBN 0-8039-6387-4 (acid-free paper).   —   ISBN 0-8039-6388-2
(pbk.: acid-free paper)
    1. Schools—Exercises and recreations—United States—Handbooks,
manuals, etc.   2. Student activities—United States—Handbooks,
manuals, etc.   3. Promotion of special events—United States—
Handbooks, manuals, etc.   I. Title.
LB3015.J37   1996
371.8'9—dc20   95-50164

This book is printed on acid-free paper.

96 97 98 99   10 9 8 7 6 5 4 3 2 1

Corwin Press Production Editor: Tricia K. Bennett

Contents

Preface

Use

This handbook is designed to improve or enhance the special events sponsored by an educational institution. The intended user of this handbook is a person who has either volunteered or been assigned to coordinate a special event for a school.

Use of this handbook will result in well-organized and successful events with measured results. Because of the processes and procedures recommended in this handbook, school administrators will be able to know the value, importance, and effectiveness of each event and to recognize the talents and abilities of those who coordinate it.

As soon as you receive this handbook, sit down in a quiet place, have a Coke or cup of coffee, and browse through the handbook in its entirety. Then you will understand what you will need to do and the ideal amount of time to allow for each step to create a very special and successful event.

You Are the Key

As the event coordinator for your school's special event, you play the most important role. You will actually make the event happen! Through your personal efforts, the event will move from a piece of paper and from within the minds of its creators into a real-life event filled with the lives of the participants and volunteers you recruit, train, and oversee.

The results of your efforts, be the event an official school function such as a graduation, a community service project, or a social activity, will translate into experiences and service that will make a difference in the lives of others. The degree of success of the event that you will coordinate depends on you. This handbook has been developed to ensure that you will be able to do your very best and achieve success.

A Tribute

This book could not have been written without the assistance of my first boss in public relations, Fred Fajardo, who handed me a well-used list of items needed for a shareholder's meeting and told me to "get them!" That was my first "big" special event, and I was allowed to see just how uptight and intense people can become about their special events.

There have been hundreds of times throughout my career in public relations and public education when I wished someone would have handed me a list that told me what I was supposed to do and what I was supposed to "get." But no such list or assistance was available for me, so I had to make them up myself and learn from my experiences.

The tips, guidelines, instructions, and forms in this book will help you succeed in the eyes of your administrators, superiors, and peers. Moreover, your efforts will be greatly appreciated by each and every person who participates in your event. Unlike some experiences in which you are unable to know the impact of your contributions on a project, an event, or people, now you will actually be able to see and hear the results of your efforts in the faces and from the lips of those who will participate in your event.

GAYLE JASSO

About the Author

Gayle Jasso has served education for more than 25 years. In 1995, she joined Baldwin Park Unified School District's Adult School as the Grants Writer. She began teaching high school English in Utah and then taught 6 more years in California before becoming a public relations executive. From 1976 to 1991, she rose to the position of First Vice President and Manager of Community Affairs for Security Pacific Corporation, the fifth largest U.S. bank holding company at the time of its merger with Bank of America in 1992.

While at Security Pacific, she created and managed over a dozen programs that served communities in six Western states. She learned special events management through her job skills training programs, which trained more than 4,500 students annually, and her volunteer programs, which involved more than 5,000 employees and retirees in the community through over 300 service projects each year. Her awards include President Reagan's 1986 Volunteer Action Award for Best Overall Corporate Effort, presented to her at the White House, and Public Relation's (PR) highest award, the Silver Anvil.

In 1991, she left Security Pacific to form a consulting business with her husband. She has written four books and nine manuals that show individuals from corporations, nonprofit organizations, and schools how to implement PR programs to enhance their organizations' reputations and their own careers.

She has an MA in English from California State University, Los Angeles, and a Professional Designation in Public Relations from UCLA. She resides in Altadena, California, with her husband, Drake, her son, David, and four Cavalier King Charles Spaniels.

1

Questions and Answers
Important Facts About Special Events

Q: What is a special event?

A: A special event is an event involving two or more people, which has a planned, very specific agenda, one or more special purposes, and one or more desired outcomes.

Q: What is the goal of a special event?

A: The goal of a special event is to provide quality events that (a) accomplish their goals and objectives, (b) are enjoyable and worthwhile for everyone who participates, and (c) use the human resources of your school and its community as coordinators, volunteers, and participants.

Q: What are the standards of a special event?

A: School special events should achieve the following standards:
- Meet real needs
- Be responsive
- Be of the highest quality
- Be efficient

- Be effective
- Be cost-effective
- Be people centered
- Be performed with sincerity
- Be performed with kindness
- Be performed with enthusiasm
- Be performed with a smile

Q: What are the elements of a quality special event?

A: Elements of a quality school event include the following:

- Important, relevant, and timely issues
- Appropriate and adequate sponsorship
- An interesting, appropriate, and convenient location
- Convenient timing
- Clear purpose and objectives
- Adequate budget to cover all expenses
- First-class staffing, including coordinators and leaders who are professional, experienced, competent, conscientious, caring, sincere, and personable
- An outstanding agenda that features top quality speakers, presenters, and entertainers as well as high-level executives and community leaders who have sterling reputations and experiences that are relevant to the purpose and issues of the special event
- Good organization and a lack of chaos
- Clear and understandable instructions and printed materials
- Interesting extracurricular activities
- Comfortable, satisfied, and enthusiastic participants

Q: Who must approve a special event?

A: Any key school or district administrator who is responsible for the event must approve it. To ensure that relevant members of a school's senior administrators are satisfied with the quality and results of a special event and, when applicable, their own participation in it, the overall event coordinator must be sure to secure necessary approval regarding key event elements. Unfortunately, there is no hard-and-fast rule regarding senior administrator approvals.

Few administrators appreciate surprises, especially when the surprise involves bad news. But providing too much information and asking for approvals too often can be viewed as bothersome and as incompetence by some key administrators, who might say, "That's what I pay you for! Don't bother me with this!" Each lead event coordinator must, therefore, learn for himself or herself where the fine line falls between what each major administrator considers too much or too little information and too many or too few requests for approval.

Q: Who are the participants of a school's special event?

A: The participants of a school event include the following:

1. *The hosts:* The hosts are the individuals responsible for the event. Examples of a host include (a) your school's principal, (b) the chief executive officer of your school's adoptive corporation, (c) your district superintendent or chancellor, (d) the president of your school board, or (e) a parent who has volunteered to chair the event. The hosts are usually not necessarily the same people who plan, implement, and oversee the event. Hosts normally attend the event and act as the official representatives to greet or welcome those who attend the event. The hosts may be representing themselves, your school or district, or an outside organization or institution. Each event should have an official host or a representative of that host to make the attendees feel comfortable and glad that they attended. If the event is very important, it should be hosted by at least one very important, high-level person who represents your school or district. The lead coordinator of the event must work closely with the host to ensure that each and every detail of the event meets with his or her approval and that the overall event will achieve its goals and accomplish its purposes.

2. *The lead coordinator:* The lead coordinator is the chief individual responsible for planning, implementing, and overseeing the event and ensuring its success. This person can be a paid staff person, a consultant, a volunteer, or even the host. This person is responsible for dealing with or supervising all providers of services required for the success of the event, such as food and beverages, entertainment, and parking.

3. *The assistant coordinators:* The assistant coordinators are the individuals who are responsible for providing any assistance necessary to the lead coordinator to ensure the success of the event. These people can also be paid staff members, consultants, volunteers, or a combination of these individuals.

4. *VIPs:* VIPs are the "very important people" from either inside or outside of your school or district. Attention must be given to every detail involving VIPs to ensure that they are treated in a

special manner; that each of their wants and needs is carefully attended to; that they are properly and appropriately seated, positioned, and introduced throughout the event; and that they are graciously and appropriately thanked for attending the event.

5. *The participants-attendees:* The people who are invited to attend and be involved in the event are the reason the event is held. Examples of participants in a school event include the following:

- School board members
- School administrators
- Parents
- Students
- Teachers
- Other staff members
- Representatives of local businesses
- Elected officials
- Residents of the school's neighborhood
- Representatives of school affiliates

Q: What are some examples of the purpose of a school special event?

A: The purposes of school events include the following:

- Community service
- Entertainment
- Appreciation
- Celebration
- Recognition
- Promotion or publicity
- Recruitment
- Training
- Graduation
- Socialization
- Networking
- Fund-raising
- Fun

Q: What are some examples of the desired outcomes of a school special event?

A: Examples of desired outcomes for school events include the following:

- Appropriate expression of gratitude, affection, or appreciation
- Improved relationships between the school or district and the individual(s) who may be attending the event
- Improved public relations
- Improved understanding and communication
- Increased loyalty
- Appropriate rewarding of outstanding achievement
- Additional income and resources
- Modified attitudes, beliefs, and behavior of everyone involved in the event

Q: What are some examples of the types of school special events?

A: Types of school events include the following:

- Community service projects
- Parties
- Receptions
- Breakfasts, luncheons, or dinners
- Fund-raisers (such as a pancake breakfast, car wash, book sale, silent auction, fashion show)
- Picnics
- Sporting events
- Awards programs
- Training programs or retreats
- Press conferences
- School board meetings
- Entertainment productions
- Graduations
- Social dances
- Academic competitions
- Contests
- Introduction of new entities (person, institution, product) to the public or school
- Celebrations of a great accomplishment, such as a new job or business, a promotion, a graduation, a new baby
- Celebrations of an important milestone, such as a birthday, anniversary, or a retirement

2

Great Expectations

What to Expect as a Special Event Coordinator

The Positive Side

As an event coordinator, you can expect to

- Grow
- Gain self-confidence
- Learn how to work with and through people
- Learn how to motivate people
- Learn how to solve problems
- Learn how to delegate and supervise tasks and responsibilities
- Learn about volunteerism from a leadership perspective (when you are overseeing volunteers)
- Feel proud of the time and effort you spend on leadership activities
- Learn about yourself
- Expand your perspectives and horizon
- Be an involved, participating citizen of your school and community

The Negative Side

These positive results will far outweigh any negative aspects of coordinating a special event; however, it is only fair to advise you of some of the difficulties you may experience. Special events create stress and risk because of their nature. Although there is no way to eliminate the stress and risk that result from special event coordination, there is one way to reduce their levels—*preparation!*

This chapter is designed to enable the individuals responsible for coordinating school special events to handle their responsibilities with minimum amounts of stress and to minimize both personal and organizational risk. Five major reasons for stress are illustrated in the following:

1. *Details:* Thousands of details must be planned and managed.
2. *People:* Many people are involved in special events as both coordinators and participants, each with his or her own presented or hidden agendas, expectations, and temperament. In addition, high-level internal and external administrators, executives, and individuals are often involved in special events. As people's titles, demands, and numbers increase, so does the intensity of the resulting stress.
3. *Pressure:* Pressure can be caused by any number of reasons, including concern, fear, worry, anxiety, time constraints, and a desire to succeed. Pressure mounts as workloads increase, deadlines draw near, emotions intensify, and prominently involved high-level administrators and individuals become more demanding as they become more concerned about and involved in the progress of the event.
4. *Complexity:* Special events are complex due to their many phases, details, and players. The only way to simplify the complexity of an event is to understand, plan, and prepare for the event.
5. *Visibility:* Special events coordination results in visibility for those responsible. Visibility is a double-edged sword. Regardless of whether the edge is positive or negative, both sides result in stress. The bad side of visibility is that individuals who are responsible for coordinating special events often feel as if everyone's eyes are on them. In a way, this feeling is accurate. If things go wrong at an event, those who are unhappy complain—usually to the highest-ranking person they can find. The overall event coordinator is the perfect and often correct scapegoat, being the person responsible for the event. The good side of visibility is that when things go right

at an event, those responsible for coordinating the event usually receive the credit and appreciation. Successful special events often result in excellent opportunities for career advancement for those who coordinated the events.

Stress Management

The following will help you manage stress and reduce its effects:

Awareness. The lead event coordinator must be aware of the nature and current status of each phase of the event, using time charts and checklists to ensure that details are being adequately addressed.

Delegation. Qualified people who understand the event's purpose, goals, objectives, and action items must be given responsibility for coordinating all or pieces of the event.

Allotments. Adequate time, staff, and resources must be allotted to prepare for, coordinate, and follow up on the event.

Techniques. Stress management techniques must be known and applied by those individuals involved in coordinating the event—for example, aerobic exercise, meditation, vacations, and time to relax.

Additional Experts. It is essential that the individuals involved in coordinating the event face their weaknesses, fears, and apprehensions, realizing their strengths and shortcomings and then seeking appropriate assistance from people who have the expertise and experience to contribute to the success of the event. Additional experts must be called in early enough in the process to be useful and to make a difference in the results.

Personal Risk

The personal risk related to a special event involves an individual's reputation as a professional, one's career opportunities (both present and future), relationships with one's family and friends (due to the time requirements of the event), and one's health (due to stress and sleep considerations if the event is inordinately time-consuming). To minimize personal risk, one must always try to remember that "this event is not the end of the world," even though it may feel as if it is. All you can do is to do your very best. Your best includes using your skills, expertise, preparation, people skills, public relations skills, and applied stress management techniques to their fullest and knowing when to ask for help if help is needed.

Organizational Risk

It helps to understand why the "higher-ups" responsible for a school event, especially an important or prestigious one, may behave the way they do when they lose their tempers, overreact, or pass their stress on to you. The following are two reasons for their stress and concern.

Reputation. A school's or district's reputation can be enhanced or damaged by the success or failure of a special event for which it is responsible or in which it is significantly involved. The possible risk of damaging an organization's reputation is minimized according to the degree with which the organization's involvement in the event has been well managed by the event's coordinators.

Liability. These days, everyone needs to be extra cautious about liability due to the overabundance of lawsuits. Special events are filled with numerous opportunities for problems and accidents that can result in liability issues. To minimize liability risks, event coordinators should contact their organization's risk management professionals for advice regarding each major event.

If you ever decide not to follow all or any part of risk management's advice, you must notify your supervisor and explain the advice you received and why you do not want to follow it. Be sure to obtain written permission to disregard the advice; otherwise, you will be personally liable if anything goes wrong.

3

The 12 Phases of a Special Event

1. *Presentation:* The proposed special event is researched and presented to the most appropriate, highest-level school or district administrators for their consideration. The goal is to receive approval for the organization to participate in or produce the event.

2. *Evaluation:* Appropriate school or district administrators evaluate the special event and decide whether it is to the organization's benefit to participate in the event.

3. *Approval:* Approval is given for the school or district to participate in or produce the event.

4. *Assignment of event coordinators:* Decisions are made as to which of the organization's departments will coordinate and oversee the event, who the overall event coordinator will be (staff member, outside consultant, or volunteer), and who will provide assistance to that individual (staff members, outside consultants, or volunteers).

5. *Planning:* The special event is planned in detail by the event coordinators. Action items are assigned to the individuals who will be responsible for them.

6. *Preparation:* Preparations are made for each and every detail relative to the special event.

7. *Setup:* At prescribed times, all physical requirements, such as audiovisual equipment, seating arrangements, signs, table settings, centerpieces, awards, place cards, and handouts, are set in place prior to the beginning of each phase of the special event.

8. *"D-Day":* The special event occurs.

9. *Teardown:* As soon as possible after the conclusion of the special event, all items that were set up and used for the event are torn down and returned to their proper places.

10. *Follow-up:* As soon as possible after the conclusion of the special event, all action and follow-up items that require attention are completed, such as thank-you notes and answers to questions.

11. *Debriefing:* The key special event coordinators, be they staff, outside consultants, or volunteers, meet together to determine the degree of success or, if applicable, failure of every major aspect of the special event.

12. *Evaluation:* Based on the debriefing session, the key special event coordinators evaluate the special event. The evaluation includes the results of the event and if and how it accomplished its objectives. The evaluation is a formal, written statement that is shared with appropriate senior administrators and kept as a resource for future event coordinators of the same or similar special events.

4

Budget Brainstorming
for Cost Management

Things to Consider

This chapter is designed to help you consider all of the important and relevant aspects of preparing a budget for your event. Each item to consider will begin with one or more questions and end with some ideas that may fit your situation or trigger other ideas that you believe should be considered in establishing the budget for your event.

Projected Costs

Q: What is the total projected cost of our school's involvement in the special event? Is the cost already included in one or more of our school's departmental budgets for the year in which the cost will be incurred? If not, how and from which budget(s) will the cost be paid? What types of costs might be incurred for this event?

A: Examples of direct and indirect costs include the following:

- Administrator time
- Staff time
- Outside consultant fees
- Marketing expenses
- Materials expenses
- Honorariums
- Rental expenses

Sources of Funds

Q: From what sources will the money come to pay for this event?

A: Possibilities for the sources of money include the following:

- Operational expenses
- Financial contributions
- In-kind contributions (an organization gives you items or services on hand or both rather than money)

History Behind This Event

Q: If our school participated in the proposed event in previous years, what was our total cost for the event each year and which departmental budgets covered the costs?

A: Examples of previous expenditures include the following:

- Hard dollars—actual outlay of dollars to cover costs
- Soft dollars—use of materials and services on hand, such as printing, office supplies, staff time
- A combination of event-related expenses from all organizational budgets that covered the total costs

Reasons for Participating

Q: Are the benefits of and reasons for participating in the event worth the total cost?

A: Examples of reasons for participating in the event include the following:

- Public relations benefits
- Community relations benefits
- Senior administrator and/or board satisfaction
- Staff satisfaction
- Student satisfaction
- Political benefits, both internal and external
- A mandatory school function

Budget Format

Q: What financial information must be included with the request-for-approval memo that will be sent to selected senior administrators from our school or district for their approval?

A: Examples of information to include are illustrated as follows:

- A total budget, broken out by standard school district categories
- Sample budgets from previous years, from our school as well as other applicable organizations, if necessary and available

Budget Approval

Q: Which administrators must give their verbal or written approval to the proposed total cost of our school's participation in the event?

A: Examples of people who should approve the budget include the following:

- The school board
- The superintendent or chancellor
- The senior administrators connected with any outside organizations that may be involved with this event
- The administrator of the department that will oversee the event if it receives approval
- The supervisor of the administrator referred to immediately above

Important Deadlines

Q: What deadlines pertain to the total cost and resultant income of the event?

A: Examples of deadlines include the following:

- Preparation of the total cost and proposed budget for the event, for approval purposes
- Payment of all incurred related event expenses
- Estimation of anticipated income from the event, such as registration fees
- Collection and distribution of income from the event

Contingency Plans

Q: If the approved event goes over budget, how will the overage be paid and from which budget(s)? What will be the consequences of going over budget?

A: Although overages could be paid from the budgets of the school or district's senior administrators who would be participating in the event or from the school or district's foundation or from the budget of the department assigned to oversee the event, there are consequences of going over budget.

Administrators may perceive those responsible for an event that goes over budget as poor managers, thus potentially limiting their opportunities for advancement. Immediate supervisors may issue performance appraisals with low ratings for the individuals responsible for an event that goes over budget, thus potentially limiting the timing and amounts of future salary increases and the number and quality of future job assignments.

The best contingency plan to have on this issue is to try every way possible not to go over budget.

Evaluation of the Budget

Q: After the event is over, the following questions should be asked to evaluate the degree of success of the budget: How will we decide whether the event was worth the total cost? Did we plan for and allocate sufficient funds to cover all costs? Did the event coordinators keep the total cost at or below the proposed budget? What format shall we use to evaluate the budget? With whom shall we share the results of our evaluation?

A: Final evaluation issues should include the following:

- A written evaluation regarding the budget and actual expenditures
- Placement of the written evaluation in the overall event evaluation package prepared at the conclusion of all phases of the event

5

The Proof Is in the Planning

Full Responsibility

As the event coordinator, you are responsible for planning, announcing, coordinating, evaluating, and measuring the success of the event you have been assigned to coordinate. That is a big task. Above all else, the success of your event will be based on how well it is planned. This chapter will take you through the essential planning steps.

Planning Meetings

A *planning meeting* can be defined as a meeting that is held either in person or by telephone to discuss and plan a special event. The purpose of a planning meeting is to decide what must be accomplished, how, when, and by whom for each phase of a special event so that the event can accomplish all of its objectives. Most events require several planning meetings.

Participants

The people who must participate in planning meetings are the lead event coordinator, assigned staff assistants, outside consultants and volunteers, and supervisors when requested or as needed. Each person must participate in a planning meeting when his or her responsibilities will be discussed. Those unable to attend must notify the lead event coordinator so that the meeting can be rescheduled if their presence is essential, and they must receive copies of the minutes of the meeting.

Agenda

Each planning meeting must have a clear, written agenda, preferably distributed prior to the meeting. Minutes must be taken of assignments given, decisions made, and the status of various aspects of the event. Copies of the minutes must be sent to all attendees, those unable to attend, and necessary supervisors immediately following each meeting.

Frequency

Planning meetings must be held whenever necessary to ensure clear communication and understanding as well as to determine the desired progress of the event. Planning meetings must not waste the time of those who attend. The appointed time and the length of time of the meetings should be convenient to a majority of the people who must attend. Planning meetings must end on schedule.

Location

The locations of the planning meetings must be politically neutral and geographically convenient for a majority of the people who must attend. Those unable to attend should be offered the option of participating on a speaker phone, if one is available, or to participate in teleconferencing, if the service is available and its cost is not prohibitive.

Duration

Planning meetings occur throughout most of the 12 phases of an event. Planning meetings begin after the proposed special event has received the approval of the organization's senior management (the approval phase) and continue as needed throughout the remaining 9 phases of special events. Planning meetings are especially important during the follow-up, debriefing, and evaluation phases so that proper decisions can be made about future participation in the event.

Time Line

A *time line* can be defined as an imaginary line laid down on a calendar to determine when tasks must be completed throughout the 12 phases of a special event. Each task must be analyzed according to how much time is required for its completion. The time line is then developed backward on a calendar starting from the date(s) of the event (D-Day).

It is hoped that ample time has been allowed to enable the coordinators to complete all required tasks throughout the phases of the event in a comfortable manner. If ample time has not been allowed, additional problems and pressures will fall on the shoulders of the coordinators in that all 12 phases of an event must be completed regardless of the amount of time that has been allowed.

The lead event coordinator, preferably with the assistance or input of all staff and outside coordinators, must develop the time line. It is best to include the major, if not all, coordinators in the development of the time line so that the time allotments for all tasks will be considerate of each coordinator's abilities and needs, while enabling each phase of the event to remain on schedule.

A copy of each revised time line should be distributed to each person who has been assigned specific responsibilities for the event, in addition to any required supervisors and involved senior administrators, if they desire this type of information. When the special event has been concluded, a master copy of the final time line should be placed in the event file for future reference for similar events and as a starting point to use again if the event is repeated. Master time lines save enormous amounts of time and effort when planning and preparing for repeated and future special events.

There is no preferred format for a time line; however, some choices include the following:

1. Writing on a calendar
2. Using a pert chart
3. Using a typed chronological listing, including headings such as these:

   Date

   Task

   Person responsible

   Completed (X)

Checklist

A *checklist* clearly itemizes brief descriptions of the tasks that must be performed so that a special event can be successfully implemented. The checklist acts as the road map and safety net for an event, ensuring that the event stays on track and that no pieces or tasks fall into the cracks or are overlooked.

A boiler plate checklist usually does not work well for a special event in that each event has numerous unique tasks that must be performed. A boiler plate checklist can serve, however, as a good starting point from which to customize a list of tasks that must be accomplished for each individual event. A sample checklist ("101 Steps to a Successful Special Event") is provided in Appendix A.

A checklist that has been developed by the lead event coordinator, preferably with the help of all assigned support staff and outside consultants, works best. Checklists must be developed and used as soon as an event has received approval from senior management.

A clearly identifiable (by date of issuance or some other equally effective and clear method), current, and updated copy of each event checklist must be kept close at hand by each person who has been assigned specific responsibilities for the event. The status of each task must be tracked on the checklist as the phases of the event evolve, change, and progress. Checklists are commonly updated during planning meetings.

When all tasks have been performed and the event has been concluded, a master copy of the checklist should be placed in the event file for future reference for similar events and as a starting point to use again if the event is repeated. Master checklists save enormous amounts of time and effort when planning and preparing for repeated and future special events.

The following elements must be included in a special event checklist:

1. Tasks
2. Responsible person(s) for each task
3. Key task phases, if a task has more than one phase
4. Responsible person(s) for each phase
5. Due dates for each phase or task
6. A space to indicate the completion of a phase or task and the date on which it was completed

Planning for Emergencies

No one knows when an emergency will occur. In that many people will be located at one spot during a special event, the chances of an accident or emergency occurring increase significantly. You should ensure that a first-aid kit is available at the event site. In addition, you should know the emergency procedures that apply to the location of your event, the procedure for contacting any security people during the event, the location of the first aid station at the event, and the address and phone numbers of the local police and fire departments. One or more staff or volunteers who are certified in cardiopulmonary resuscitation (CPR) should be recruited to attend and be on call during the event.

When the Event Must Be Canceled

If it becomes necessary to cancel the event, you must ensure that each person who signed up to help coordinate the event is called at least 2 hours prior to the earliest arrival time you indicated in your confirmation package. These assistants can be invaluable to help you notify the attendees as soon as it is learned that the event must be canceled. This notification will be possible if you make sure to include a daytime and evening phone number (complete with area codes) on the enrollment or RSVP forms.

6

A Dozen Brainstorming
Modules for Success

How to Use These Modules

Scan and Select

Before you begin planning your event, scan the titles of the following 12 modules. Then read the modules that you believe will pertain to your event. If your event is significant and complex, perhaps all 12 modules will apply. You can skip the modules that contain information that will not apply to smaller and simpler events. The information included in these modules will enable you and your school to produce successful special events on any scale and for any group of participants—from a simple party in a private home to a major, international conference culminating in a formal dinner at the White House.

Think of each of these modules as a brainstorming session filled with ideas, questions, and examples. The information presented in each module will give you a solid foundation of subject knowledge. Equally important, the information will stimulate additional ideas that will apply to you, your situation, and your school's special events. Use the modules and their information in whatever way will help you to produce a successful and outstanding event. If each module triggers just one important idea that will make your event more outstanding and successful, then it will have accomplished its purpose!

Module 1: Agenda

The Agenda Is the "Draw"

The agenda is one of the most important parts of a special event in that it attracts people and turns them into attendees, participants, and presenters. As the event coordinators plan the agenda, they need to decide (a) what experiences they want the attendees to have from the time they start their trip to the event to the time they return home, (b) how they want the event to influence the attendees, (c) what they want the attendees to learn as a result of their participation in the event, and (d) what opinions they want the attendees to form as a result of the attendees' experiences during the event.

Purposes

Examples of the purposes of an agenda for a special event include the following:

- Information and instruction
- Motivation and inspiration
- Networking and socializing
- Entertainment and refreshment
- Celebration of a milestone, such as graduation or retirement

History

If this event has occurred previously, event coordinators must research every possible aspect of it, including (a) what items were on the agenda; (b) how the agenda was evaluated by the former attendees, participants, and presenters; (c) the agenda items that should be repeated; and (d) possible new items to add.

Examples of historical issues regarding a special event include the following:

- A general analysis of previous agendas, if available, carefully comparing them with the goals and objectives established for the proposed new event
- A review of previous attendees', participants', and presenters' evaluation forms and the final evaluation reports prepared by previous event coordinators
- Interviews with previous key event attendees, participants, and presenters as well as members of the school and district's key administrators and each cosponsor's senior management who were involved in previous events in major capacities

Elements Contributing to Success

To ensure that this event is an outstanding success, decisions must be made and steps must be taken early in the planning process. Examples of elements that should be considered as possible contributors to the overall success of the event include the following:

- The skills of professional meeting planners
- The skills of professional speech writers
- The skills of professional speakers
- The use of only those speakers, trainers, and entertainers who have proven credentials and experience (as verified by other coordinators)
- The participation of high-level, well-known, and influential individuals as sponsors, chairpersons, advisers, and program participants
- Proper and sufficient research on previously held events
- The appointment of only the best qualified, most experienced individuals as event coordinators

Things to Consider to
Please School Administrators

Ultimately, the perceived success of a special event rests with the school and district administrators whose reputations are at risk when it is decided that their school will host a particular event. The following are some examples of specific items that are regarded as important by school and district administrators in addition to executives of corporations that also may be involved as cosponsors:

- Adherence to budget limitations
- Allowance of ample time to plan the agenda
- Allowance of enough time to secure commitments from desired program participants and presenters
- A clear and important purpose for the event
- Positive and supportive attitudes of the key administrators as well as of senior management from other event cosponsors toward the event
- An appropriate tone for the event
- Positive feedback from the event attendees and the program participants from previous events
- The involvement of key administrators from the school and district as well as senior executives from other event cosponsors in planning, approving, and participating in the agenda
- Clearly defined desired outcomes for the school, for the event, for other cosponsors, for the event's attendees, and for the program's participants and presenters

The Four Types of Agendas

For clarification purposes, throughout the remainder of this module, the agenda will be referred to by using four different terms, each with a different meaning.

General Agenda

The *general agenda* is the overall agenda concept, previously referred to as the *agenda*. Specific agenda components include the following:

- Issues and topics
- VIPs and celebrities
- Keynote speakers
- General sessions (all attendees together): masters of ceremonies, speakers, moderators, discussion leaders, and panelists
- Breakout sessions (attendees divided into groups): speakers, presenters, trainers, moderators, and panelists

- Planned program activities
- Meals and refreshments
- Entertainment
- Special activities for spouses
- Extracurricular activities
- Transportation

Proposal Agenda

The *proposal agenda* can be defined as a description of the general agenda plan, which includes the minimum amount of information required by the people who must review a proposal for a special event to enable them to make a decision about whether their organization(s) should participate in the event. A proposal agenda may be a simple, brief outline of possible agenda items or it may be a well-developed draft of either the working agenda or the participant agenda (see the following sections), depending on the tastes and requirements of those who must approve the event. The proposal agenda is completed after the general agenda has been sufficiently developed for approval.

Working Agenda

The *working agenda* can be defined as a comprehensive, detailed road map of the general agenda plan that is used by each event coordinator to ensure that the event achieves its final goal—a successful, well-organized, effective, and efficient special event. The working agenda includes the following general information:

1. The event's name
2. The event's dates
3. The event's location
4. The event's sponsor(s)
5. The event's purpose, goals, and objectives

Moreover, each item of a working agenda contains the following components:

1. The date of the working agenda item
2. The starting and ending time, including the total number of hours and minutes required to accomplish the working agenda item (e.g., 9:00 a.m. to 11:30 a.m. or 2.5 hours)

3. The location of the working agenda item, such as the fourth-floor conference room

4. The name and description of each working agenda item, including the names of the program participants (e.g., "Welcome Reception," hosted by the sponsor's chief executive officer, with entertainment provided by the local university's jazz band)

5. The names of the event coordinator(s) responsible for accomplishing the working agenda item

6 The physical requirements of the working agenda item, including their sources, scheduled delivery times and locations, and installation dates and times

The first draft of the working agenda must be completed as soon as possible after the proposal agenda and the school's participation in the event have been approved and in time to contact all proposed program participants and presenters to receive their commitments to participate. The working agenda must be kept current by filling in gaps with confirmed details and information as they become available and by reflecting changes from previous versions of the working agenda on current and dated drafts.

Attendee Agenda

The *attendee agenda* can be defined as the printed copy of the general agenda plan that each attendee receives at the beginning of the event. The attendee agenda consists of the following components:

- The basic event information that the attendees must know
- Clearly written, easy-to-understand language enhanced by quality design elements
- A clear and logical manner of presentation

The attendee agenda is not developed until all working agenda details are finalized and it is time for the attendee agenda to be presented to the designer and printer.

Printing Considerations for the Attendee Agenda. The following are items that must be decided regarding the printing of the attendee agenda:

1. Type

Typewriter (not recommended unless there are no other options)

Computer

Professional typesetting

Style of type (type face)

2. Design

The best person to design the attendee agenda must be selected from inside or outside of the school or district

Graphics

Layout

Quality, style, and color of paper

Color(s) of ink

3. Printing equipment

Photocopy machine

Off-set printing, using either an internal or external print shop

Printing press, using either an internal or external print shop

4. Lead time requirements: A determination must be made of the minimum and maximum amounts of lead time required to receive the printed attendee agendas on schedule and in time to mail or distribute them as planned.

5. Delivery: The specifics of delivery of the printed attendee agendas must be determined, including how, when, where, and to whom the copies will be delivered.

Distributing Considerations for the Attendee Agenda. There are several options for distributing the attendee agenda to the attendees, including the following:

- A copy of the printed attendee agenda could be included in each attendee's confirmation materials.
- A copy of the printed attendee agenda could be included in each attendee's packet.
- A copy of the printed attendee agenda could be given to each attendee at the check-in or registration area.
- A copy of the printed attendee agenda could be placed at each attendee's seat.
- A system must be developed to determine how additional copies of the printed attendee agenda will be distributed, if any are requested.

Approvals

The lead event coordinator must obtain the names and titles of all of the people, both from inside and from outside of the school and district, who must approve the working agenda before proposed program participants and presenters can be contacted to secure their participation. The following are examples of the people who must approve the proposal agenda and proposed program participants and presenters of a special event:

- Senior administrators from the school and district and from any cosponsoring organizations
- The head of the department responsible for overseeing the event
- Any supervisor above the coordinator or overseer who they believe should approve the working agenda

Dealing With Changes in the Agenda

Changes in the agenda can be accommodated up to the time when the attendee agenda is in the design and typesetting phases, although changes at these late stages increase costs. When an attendee agenda goes to the printer, however, the agenda is final. The only way to correct it is to reprint it. Even if the budget can accommodate the increased cost, there may not be enough time to reprint an attendee agenda. In that reprinting doubles the cost allocated to printing, a decision to reprint an attendee agenda must be made by the head of the school department responsible for overseeing the event.

Contingency Plans

People attend special events because of the proposed and advertised agendas. Because emergencies do occur that affect the scheduled participants and presenters of an agenda of an event, the following provides examples of people who could be asked to be prepared to step in if anyone should have to cancel on the program:

- The key school and district administrators and other event sponsors
- Representatives of those administrators and event sponsors
- Entertainers or VIPs who have a relationship with the school or district or any of the event cosponsors

- Members of the staff from the school department assigned to oversee the event who have related, quality expertise and excellent presentation skills
- Appropriate staff members from any of the event sponsors who have related, quality expertise and excellent presentation skills
- Outside consultants and professional speakers with whom the school or district has worked and who might be available on short notice

Evaluating the Agenda

The agenda can be evaluated by asking the following questions: Did the event's final working agenda occur as planned? Was the event successful overall? Was each working agenda item successful? Why or why not? The following are examples of ways to evaluate the degree of success of a special event's agenda:

- Errors or unplanned incidents that created problems and lowered expected outcomes (and their causes) must be identified.
- Evaluations from event attendees, participants, and presenters, both written and oral, must be obtained.
- Feedback from the school's and district's key administrators and board members who were involved in the event must be sought, if necessary and appropriate.
- Feedback from the senior managers of other event cosponsors who were involved in the event must be sought, if necessary and appropriate.

Module 2: Ambiance

Ambiance can be defined as one's surrounding atmosphere and environment. Positive ambiance is to a special event what chocolate mint frosting is to a cake.

Positive Ambiance

Positive ambiance influences attitudes and behavior in a positive manner. For example, when event coordinators are cordial and responsive, when the event is located in a quality site, when event decorations and promotional items are well designed and attractive, and when food is delicious and beautifully served, the positive ambiance often causes participants to perceive an average or good event as outstanding.

Negative Ambiance

Conversely, negative ambiance influences attitudes and behavior in a negative manner. For example, when an event's participants are in any way inconvenienced or made to feel uncomfortable, when the surroundings and accommodations are substandard and unattractive, and when the event's decorations and promotional items do not have a quality appearance, the negative ambiance often causes participants to perceive a good event as average and an average event as poor.

Contributors to Positive Ambiance

The following are items that contribute to positive ambiance:

- An event site that is located in an interesting and well-known city with diverse people and interests
- Tasteful, well-appointed facility decor
- A clever event theme
- An appealing event color scheme
- Artistically designed printed materials
- Quality printed materials
- Delicious and varied food served in an appealing manner, including a menu that can accommodate the special dietary requirements of all participants
- An appropriate dress code
- Creative and clever decorations and centerpieces
- Thematic promotional items
- Unique gifts and door prizes
- Original awards and recognition items
- Suitable music
- Outstanding entertainment
- State-of-the-art audiovisual equipment
- Expert technicians
- Appropriate sound levels for the audience

- Pleasant, responsive, and attentive event coordinators
- Exceptional, prompt, helpful, and personable service
- Clearly posted, nicely printed signs informing participants where and when event items are occurring
- Easy-to-read and attractive name badges, affixed in a manner that does not damage clothing and that can be easily removed and put on another garment
- Interesting, unusual, and exciting extracurricular activities
- Accessible, convenient transportation around the buildings or area of the event site
- Comfortable temperatures in all meeting and hotel rooms
- Prompt and sincere thank-you notes, responses to questions, and responses to special requests

Budget Considerations

Budget constraints affect an event's ambiance. Because of the importance of ambiance, event coordinators must do everything possible to stretch the budget creatively. By carefully checking references, seeing samples of work, and obtaining bids on specific projects and jobs, event coordinators can enlist the services of exceptionally talented people who use top-grade materials in their work at reasonable fees, enabling the event to be of the highest quality while staying within its budget.

Political Considerations

Any decision regarding ambiance can be perceived both negatively and positively depending on the perspective of the critic. As the saying goes, "You can't please all of the people all of the time." Political considerations, therefore, must be kept in mind regarding decisions that contribute to ambiance. The following items provide political considerations that should be addressed.

Cost

Q: Does it look as if the event is too expensive or too cheap?

Too expensive: It appears that most of the participants' financial contributions to a school's fund-raiser have been spent on the meal, the entertainment, and the centerpieces, causing the participants to have second thoughts about the wisdom of having contributed to this particular school.

Too cheap: The event is so cheaply handled that it makes the sponsor(s) appear to be cheap, to be less than first-class, and possibly to be experiencing financial difficulties.

Location

Q: Does the location fit the nature of the event and the perspectives of the participants?

For example, a luxurious high-rise has been selected to host a back-to-school training day for the teachers from the local junior high school located in the inner city. Rather than perceiving the corporation as a good corporate citizen and being grateful for the corporation's generosity, the teachers believe the corporation is trying to show them "how the other half lives." The result is that a group of the teachers sends a letter to the chief executive officer of the corporation asking that the corporation share some of its profits with the public schools in general and their school in particular.

Tone

Q: Is the event being handled in a manner that will be perceived as appropriate for its purpose?

For example, an event that has been created for children is being run as if the children were sophisticated adults. Consequently, the children are bored and restless, and their parents are unhappy with the event and its sponsor.

Attention to Detail

Q: Is everything well organized, or are there numerous loose ends?

Disorganized: Because the event coordinators have announced several program and meeting room changes throughout the event, many of the participants have become noticeably confused and annoyed.

Loose ends: Handouts are not available when they are supposed to be, the awards are not in place prior to the participants entering the meeting hall, and many of the participants have started complaining about the unprofessionalism of the event.

Sometimes You Just Can't Win

> **Q:** Are the event coordinators so good that maybe they are *too good?*

For example, the lead event coordinator has all of the thousands of details of the event so well managed and so well organized and has done such a superb job of training and preparing the assistant event coordinators that members of the school's and district's senior administrators wonder why so many of the district's staff members have been assigned to coordinate the event. Rather than being impressed with the management skills of the event coordinators, administrators believe the district is wasting money on salaries for unnecessary staff members and fees for unnecessary consultants.

Appropriateness

> **Q:** Are the elements of the event (such as the speakers, their subjects and points of view, the entertainment, and the dress code) appropriate for the occasion and the event sponsor(s)?

For example, the keynote speaker, who is a prominent chief executive officer from a major local corporation and who refused to provide a copy of his speech for approval prior to his presentation, includes political views in his speech that have nothing to do with the purpose of the event. Consequently, many members of the audience are offended.

Module 3: Announcements

Invitations

The style of invitation must suit the budget, the event's purpose, the event's importance, the status of the event, and the status of the invited guests. The event's theme should be incorporated into the words and the color scheme should be incorporated into the design if the budget will accommodate more than one color in the printing process. The invitation package must include the following items:

1. The invitation and outside mailing envelope
2. An RSVP form with a self-addressed, stamped return envelope
3. A map with clear directions and parking instructions

   4. A parking pass, if there will be a charge for parking and the budget can accommodate covering the parking expenses for the participants

   5. A ticket or tickets, if applicable

Additional Announcements

Depending on the nature and purpose of the event, additional announcements can include the following:

- Paid advertisements
- Public service spots
- Publicity, using both internal and external media
- Posters
- Table tents
- Statement stuffers
- Banners
- Special requests made by the manager of the department that is overseeing the event or the event coordinator asking executives to solicit participation in the event

Tickets

If tickets are to be sold to the event, a system must be devised to

1. Print the tickets
2. Sell the tickets
3. Collect and securely hold the money
4. Transport the money
5. Deposit the money (into what bank account?)
6. Audit the money
7. Distribute the money to its final destination(s) or budget(s)
8. Distribute the tickets to the attendees
9. Collect the event tickets at the registration table, at the door, at the ticket office, at the meal table, or at another convenient location more suitable to the nature and site of the event

Because there are so many aspects of ticket sales with which to be concerned, it may be advisable to turn the ticket sales over to an outside company that specializes in the sale, distribution, and collection of tickets and in the secure handling of all monies.

Confirmations

Some events require that written confirmations be sent to the guests who have said they will be attending. The confirmation package may include the following:

- A letter of confirmation that includes essential details about the event, including the arrival time and place
- Additional information for participants who identified their special needs—such as handicapped parking and access or special dietary restrictions—explaining how those needs will be addressed and accommodated during the event
- A map with clear directions and parking instructions
- A parking pass
- A ticket or tickets

Module 4: Arrivals and Departures

We're Here!

The day has finally come. The participants will soon be arriving and be ready to begin experiencing the special event that has drawn them to the site selected by the coordinators. Many of the participants will be tired, anxious, and stressed when they arrive. The event coordinators must help the arriving participants feel welcome and comfortable.

Arrival Instructions

Included in the participants' original invitations or confirmation packets must be clear arrival instructions. Some of the kinds of questions that the participants will ask and that must be answered in the information they receive before they arrive are presented in the following sections.

Arriving by Car

Q: How do I get there? Where do I park? How do I find the parking structure or parking lot? How much is it going to cost me to park? Must I have cash, or will the parking attendants be able to put the charges on my bill or credit card?

> **A:** Provide the participants with a clearly drawn or copied map of the area, including freeway exit instructions and arrows drawn from access streets right to the entrance of the parking area. Include special explanatory notes if there are confusing streets or turns and if there are key indicators that can let the participants know that they are getting close and are on the right track, such as a McDonald's or special landmark. Also, include a parking pass if the budget can accommodate the expense. Be sure to tell the participants exactly where to park in the structure or in the lot if a special level or section has been reserved for the event's use. At the entrance to the parking area, place a sign with the name of the event clearly printed in large, easy-to-read letters.

Additional Considerations. If a large number of participants are expected to arrive by car, especially around the same time, it may be a good idea to contact the local police department and advise them of the possible significant increase in traffic. The police may be able to assist in many ways, including suggesting alternate routes.

Arriving by Air

> **Q:** How do I get from the airport to the event site? How far is the airport from the site? How much will it cost me to get there?
>
> **A:** Tell the participants how many miles the airport is from the event site and how much time they should allow to travel from the airport to the site at various times of day, allowing for changes in traffic flow. Provide options for ground transportation, such as a taxi, bus, complimentary hotel bus or limousine, private limousine, or special event shuttle bus. Provide approximate costs, including tipping information. If the event is providing a shuttle bus, be sure that the bus is clearly marked with a sign naming the event in large, easy-to-read letters, and be sure to include the departure schedule for the bus.

Additional Solutions. If a large group of participants is expected to arrive on the same plane, it may be a good idea to have someone meet the group and help them get their luggage and find their way to the event site.

Handicapped Arrivals

> **Q:** I am a quadriplegic in a wheelchair. What do I do and where do I go to get into the hotel and get around during the event?

A: If the regular arrival procedures and areas at the airport and at the event site cannot accommodate people who have physical handicaps, then the event coordinators must research how the needs of people who have physical handicaps can be accommodated. Examples of information that must be discovered include special entrances and rooms that can accommodate wheelchairs and special parking structure entrances that can accommodate extra tall vehicles. If, prior to sending out the event announcements, the event coordinators know of any event participants who will have special needs, their special arrival instructions must be included in the event announcements. The special instructions must also be included in the information sent to the people who have said they will be attending.

Hospitality

A well-marked, "friendly" hospitality table is a crucial element of managing event arrivals. Hospitality services include welcoming, directing, providing information, answering questions, and providing research about special questions. Prior to and throughout the event, a special hospitality table must be set up and staffed by friendly and knowledgeable event coordinators. The hospitality table must be put in a prominent and easy-to-find area of the event site. Depending on the circumstances and logistics of each event, the hospitality table may or may not be the same as the registration table.

Check-In Instructions

At the Hotel

Information. If an event is being held at a hotel or if a particular hotel is being recommended to the event's participants, event information should include special check-in instructions to help speed up the hotel registration process and enable the participants to find their rooms quickly and with the least amount of effort. Recommendations for alternate hotels should be included in the event information for participants who do not register early enough to secure a room at the suggested hotel or for those who prefer to stay at a hotel away from the event site.

Early Arrivals. If the event begins early in the morning, many participants prefer to arrive the afternoon or evening of the day before. To accommodate their needs and help them feel welcome, provide a welcome reception where the early arrivals can meet people and form groups for dinner. Recommendations for restaurants for that first evening are always appreciated by the participants.

At the Event

The location of the registration table for the event must be clearly posted in the lobby and on elevator message boards at the event site. The registration table must be clearly marked with large signs indicating the name of the event and its sponsor. It is essential that the event registration table be adequately staffed by knowledgeable, friendly, and courteous people who can quickly locate each participant's registration information, such as tickets and packets. If a large number of participants are expected, the event coordinators must organize a processing system that ensures short lines and brief waiting times.

Greeters and Event Hosts

At the beginning of the event, arriving participants appreciate friendly, easily identified greeters who provide firsthand information about the event, even if the information is the same as the information that was sent to participants (but that may have remained unread).

Greeters help participants feel welcome, comfortable, and confident about where to go and what to do. Throughout the event, participants continue to have questions. Easily identifiable event hosts with excellent people skills and a thorough understanding of event details are greatly appreciated by the participants.

Latecomers

Plans must be made to accommodate the questions and needs of the participants who arrive late. Latecomers should be able to join the group quickly and with the least amount of distraction to the other participants and the least amount of embarrassment to themselves.

Departures

Departures begin when the participants start to leave, which may or may not be when the last item on the agenda is over. The same quantity and quality of attention and service provided by event coordinators to arriving participants must be provided to the participants as they leave, ensuring a continuity of care and concern.

Instructions

Instructions for departures and check-out must be included in the participants' packets and announced during the program when necessary to ensure that no participants become frustrated or confused during their departures.

Late Departures

Event coordinators must be aware that some participants, for business or personal reasons, may remain at the event site for a period of time after the conclusion of the event. Event coordinators must be available to provide assistance to participants for as long as the coordinators remain at the event site. Prior to leaving the event site themselves, the event coordinators must do their best to attend to the special needs of the known participants who will be remaining at the site after the conclusion of the event.

Hotel Check-Out Instructions

Arrangements must be made with the hotel for fast and simple check-out procedures, secure storage of participants' luggage prior to departure, and an extension of room hours for those who must remain in the hotel a few additional hours but not an additional night.

Airport Transportation

If the event provided an airport shuttle bus for arriving participants, the event should provide an airport shuttle bus at the conclusion of the event—with the same courtesy.

Last Impressions

Last impressions are often as important to event participants as first impressions. Event coordinators must sustain the quality and level of attention to the needs of participants until the last participant has driven away or boarded the plane for home. Then, and only then, is the event officially over and ready to be analyzed and evaluated.

Module 5: Attendees

Deciding Who Should Come

One of the first steps to take in a special event is to determine who the target public (the groups of people) is going to be—who will be invited to attend the event. It is essential to determine the attendees *before* you develop the agenda. Examples of potential attendees include the following:

- Corporate representatives
- Community representatives
- Civic and professional organization representatives
- Political representatives
- Representatives from a specific age, ethnic, or economic group
- The general public
- Members of the school's and district's senior administrators
- Employees or retirees of the school and district
- Friends of the school and district or its particular representatives
- Students and associates of the school and district or its particular representatives

Types of Attendees

One of the best ways to help you decide who to invite is to find out who attended the event in previous years. Find out if the participation of various groups and individuals who attended was necessary and successful. The names of previous attendees can be found on copies of previous guest lists if they are available. Those lists should be obtained, analyzed, and discussed.

After you have analyzed and discussed previous guest lists, ask yourself if there are any other individuals or representatives of special groups who should be invited. Examples of additional types of people who might be invited include the following:

- Celebrities
- Politicians and city officials
- Public service representatives
- Personal friends
- Relatives
- Representatives of other educational institutions
- Potential students

Handling Hidden and Subtle Agendas

You will need to discover if there are any hidden or subtle agendas or relationships that must be considered to avoid embarrassment or awkward situations during the event. Some examples of these include people who have physical handicaps, divorced couples, private or confidential personal relationships, strong likes or dislikes of individuals or groups, family problems, competitors, friends, and enemies. Examples of steps you can take to ensure that everyone is comfortable include the following:

- Special seating arrangements
- Special traffic flow arrangements
- Special entrances and exits

Developing the Invitation List for Approval

You must pull together the names, titles, and affiliations of the people being proposed for the guest list for this event. Then you will need to determine which, if any, names should be included in the request-for-approval memo to the appropriate and necessary key senior school and district administrators for their verbal or written approval to the proposed guest list. Examples of the people who may need to approve the guest list include (a) the school and district key senior administrators who are connected with the sponsoring or benefiting organizations, (b) the head of the department assigned to oversee the event, and (c) the supervisor of that department head.

The method of preparing the list of potential attendees could include a list of the target public to be invited and why, or it could be a list of the individuals and their affiliations (or groups of people to be invited) and why they should be invited.

The Revised and
Approved Guest List

A revised guest list, reflecting the input and necessary approval from administrators, must be made and added to the list or entered into the computer for immediate use. You will need to decide who should coordinate the development of the guest list, its approval, and the input of the list into the computer. An ideal person would be a staff member who is excellent with detail, accuracy, and the computer, or one who has access to a secretary who has these skills. (Errors must not be made on the guest list, invitations, and RSVPs!)

The deadline for completing the guest list must be set as soon as possible after approvals have been received to allow sufficient time to mail the invitations and enable the invitees to enter the event on their calendars and then to RSVP. Allowing too much time is unwise because the invitees often set the invitation aside and forget about the event, thinking there is plenty of time to attend to the invitation later. Allowing too little time results in possible calendar conflicts for the invitees and too short of notice for receiving the RSVPs and confirming necessities such as food, meeting rooms, hotel accommodations, and travel arrangements.

Contingency Plans

An alternate list of guests should be developed in order of priority in case some or too many of the original invitees are unable to attend and in case the smaller group would be an embarrassment for the school, district, and other cosponsors. (It is always wise to have some people in mind who can be available on short notice to fill tables if necessary.)

Evaluation

After the event has concluded, all event coordinators should determine if the guest list that was developed resulted in the type and number of attendees anticipated. The following list contains four ways you can analyze your guest list:

1. An analysis can be performed of the percentage of positive RSVPs, making special note of the individuals the school or district really wanted to attend.

2. An analysis can be performed of the number of people who did not attend at the last minute, although they said they would, to attempt to determine why they did not come.

3. An analysis can be performed of the event evaluation forms, looking for indications that the type of attendees who were invited actually enjoyed the event and were well suited to its purpose and activities.

4. Personal and private phone calls can be made to close friends and associates who attended the event to assess their feelings about and experiences during the event.

Module 6: Communication Systems

Definition

A *communication system* can be defined as any action, organizational process, individual piece of equipment, or network of equipment that facilitates communication. Communication systems make it possible for people in charge of events to communicate easily and quickly with one another and for participants to send and receive messages as needed. Effective communication systems lessen the stress and confusion that often accompany special events.

Communication Needs

Communication systems are important in that they enable event coordinators to facilitate the communication needs of all event and program participants during normal, routine circumstances as well as during emergencies. The selection of communication systems for an event is determined by the following:

- Each event's communication requirements
- The communication systems available in the facilities located at the event site
- The degree of remoteness of the location's community or geographic area
- The event's size, complexity, and number of anticipated participants
- The status and security needs of the participants
- The necessity of event coordinators to be in constant contact with one another throughout an event

Technicians

Experienced and skilled technicians or school or district representatives must deliver and properly install each piece of communication equipment and each communication system. Depending on the complexity of the equipment and systems, the technicians or school technical representatives must either train event coordinators to operate the equipment and systems correctly or operate the equipment and systems themselves during the event. Each person responsible for any aspect of the communication systems for an event must be responsible, competent, well trained, knowledgeable about the equipment and operational procedures, and comfortable with the importance of these responsibilities.

Rental

State-of-the-art communication equipment and systems are expensive to own, and many must be installed in buildings and vehicles. Unless a school has an ongoing need for the specific communication systems and equipment required for a particular event and unless a school has the capability of transporting the equipment to and from each event site, it is preferable to rent communication equipment and systems from either the event site's facility or from competent companies with reputations for quality equipment and technical expertise.

Equipment rental is recommended because special events vary in size, complexity, and locations. In addition, equipment becomes outdated quickly and to be effective, communication systems must be custom-tailored to each situation.

Communication Systems Examples

Communication systems vary according to need, complexity, sophistication, and availability. Some examples of communication systems are listed in the following:

- A staffed information center to handle communication, emergencies, first aid, dispatching, registration, and lost and found
- Secretarial support
- Messenger services or runners
- Chalkboards or message boards at key central locations

- Clearly written materials containing information about the event
- Office equipment (including manual and battery operated or manual in case of power outages), such as typewriters, computers, and copiers
- A master list of event participants and their phone numbers
- A master list of emergency phone numbers, such as the local police, fire department, paramedics, search and rescue services, hospitals, and on-call emergency clinics
- Sign-in and sign-out rosters
- Identification badges
- Bull horns
- Whistles
- AM/FM radios with weather channels
- Land line telephones
- Voice mail systems to centralize event information
- Answering machines
- Personal hotel room message capability, such as a telephone and a television with computerized messages
- Fax machines
- Pocket pagers, localized or citywide depending on requirements
- Cellular phones
- Two-way, handheld radios with spare batteries and chargers
- Marine radios
- Shared access to use the local authorities' two-way radio system for emergencies
- Signers for the hearing impaired
- Signs to indicate entrances, parking, rest rooms, handicapped facilities, meeting areas, and meeting topics or presenters

Important Considerations

This chapter discusses communication systems in depth. Knowing how to select and work with communication systems technicians is as important as knowing how to select the best and most suitable communication equipment. When you are working on the communication systems portion of an event, after you have read this module, kindly turn to "Module 8: Physical Requirements" and read it in its entirety. Module 8 includes many ideas and perspectives to assist you as you work with technicians.

Module 7: Meals

Mouth Over Matter

The way to an event participant's heart is through his or her stomach. How a particular meal strikes a person's fancy often remains in his or her mind and is a topic of conversation far beyond how well he or she liked the keynote speaker. In addition, opportunities for eating and drinking enable participants to network, socialize, and converse. These social opportunities are often as important to the participants, if not more important, than the event's nonsocial agenda.

Food and Beverage Considerations

Catering Manager Issues

- Is the manager's office located on-site?
- Is the manager readily available to help in the planning and serving of the meals and refreshments throughout the event?
- Is the manager responsive to all requests and needs?
- Is the manager courteous to all event coordinators and participants?
- Is the manager professional in appearance and actions?
- Is the manager a problem solver or a problem maker?
- Does the manager have an excellent and well-trained staff?

Timing Issues

- Periods when refreshments should be provided
- Frequency of eating and drinking
- Open eating arrangement versus having a set beginning and end for each meal or refreshment period

Style Issues

- Informal versus formal
- Open versus reserved seating
- Buffet versus sit-down
- Free conversation versus working meal or formal program

Menu Issues

- Type of food
- Variety of food
- Freshness of food
- Uniqueness of food
- Quality of food
- Number of courses
- Food that is appropriate and related to the theme of the event
- The chef's ability to accommodate special dietary requirements for participants with special needs
- The availability and desirability of wine and alcoholic beverages (What is the school or district's philosophy/policy on serving alcoholic beverages relative to issues such as liability, reputation, and appropriateness?)
- A host- or a no-host bar (How will a no-host bar be perceived and received by the participants?)

Service Issues

- Speed
- Quietness
- Courteousness
- Responsiveness
- Safety (first aid and CPR)
- Communication (in predominant languages spoken by the event participants)

Types of Eating or Drinking Situations

- Continental breakfast
- Full breakfast—buffet or sit-down
- Coffee or beverage break, with or without snacks
- Luncheon—buffet or sit-down
- Formal afternoon tea
- Reception with cocktails, beverages, or hors d'oeuvres
- Dinner—buffet or sit-down
- After dinner, late evening beverage or reception service

Locations

- Foyers
- Dining or meeting rooms
- Private dining rooms
- Private individual participant rooms

Room or Table Arrangements

- Round tables
- Rectangular tables, separated or joined in prescribed configurations, such as U-shaped or square
- Head tables
- Chairs in rows, with no tables
- Chairs around the edges of the room, with no tables
- Accommodations for extra people who do not have reservations
- Linen service to accommodate the event's color scheme
- China, crystal, and silver selection availability
- Space for a bar
- Space for a program and entertainment
- Space to store and secure personal items and equipment in the meal room

Storage and Security Considerations

- Wardrobes for coats and umbrellas, with locks, if necessary, placed in foyers and entrances
- Lockers or a coat check service
- Security guards to guard valuable coats during meals, programs, and social activities

Program Accommodations

- Dance floor
- Dais or podium
- Lectern with light and microphone
- Head table(s)
- Special lighting
- Sound system and technician

- Stage
- Space for band, orchestra, or entertainers
- Audiovisual equipment and technician(s)
- Eating or rehearsal room(s) for speakers, musicians, and entertainers

Set-Up Issues

- Sufficient time
- Sufficient help
- Reception table
- Seating chart or system
- Name badges
- Decorations
- Centerpieces
- Table numbers, large posted maps, and identification cards to facilitate prompt, orderly seating
- Programs, gifts, and place cards
- Special room arrangements
- Sufficient time for rehearsals of speakers and entertainers
- Sufficient time to test the sound and lighting systems

Additional Staffing Issues

- Receptionists
- Ushers
- Security guards

Special Needs Issues

- Accommodation of early arrivals
- Accommodation of bodyguards
- Accommodation of VIP escorts
- Emergency or evacuation procedures
- Private entrances and exits for VIPs
- Security screening or clearances of all guests entering the meal room, if necessary
- Special accommodations for the handicapped
- Special accommodations for the media

- Plans for accommodating people who arrive late
- Food and beverage service for program participants and entertainers

Module 8: Physical Requirements

Definition

Physical requirements can be defined as tangible items that are needed to implement the agenda and accomplish the purposes of a special event.

Planning

After the event's agenda has been planned, the event coordinators must analyze the agenda, piece by piece, to determine what physical requirements will be needed so that each item on the agenda can occur as planned and can accomplish its objectives.

There are always choices to be made regarding brand names, quality, accessibility, cost, and technical assistance required for each physical need. Decisions must be made according to the available budget and the minimum standard of quality that will be considered as acceptable by the members of senior management of the event's sponsor(s), the school's and district's key administrators, and the event's major and most prestigious participants.

Assigned Coordinators

The person(s) assigned to oversee the physical requirements of a special event must be excellent in handling detail; must be able to plan and manage time well, allowing for overlaps and delays; and must be able to solve problems as they occur, such as equipment that will not work properly. Event coordinators have many responsibilities pertaining to the physical requirements of an event.

Ordering

After the physical needs of the event have been determined, the coordinators must decide how best to acquire the items, whether to rent or purchase them and from what sources, and how to stay within the budget and still achieve the desired quality standard established for the event.

Event Site

It is common for event sites to have catering managers, audiovisual technicians, and other event specialists who can provide many if not all of the required items, equipment, and operational and repair service. In fact, the availability of necessary items, equipment, and experts is one of the primary selection criteria of a site for an event. Sometimes, however, as in the case of a quality sound and lighting system, the event site cannot provide the equipment or technicians that can guarantee the required level of quality and results.

Alternative Sources

If the event site cannot provide the necessary equipment, supplies, repair service, and operating technicians, then the event coordinators must locate companies in the surrounding area of the site that can provide the items and service needed. If the local businesses cannot provide them, then the coordinators must arrange to either transport necessary equipment, supplies, and technicians to the event site or make arrangements with a known company to deliver them to or provide them at the event site.

Delivering

Coordinators must ensure that the items are transported and delivered undamaged and on schedule.

Installing

Coordinators must ensure that the items and equipment are correctly and safely set up or installed in their proper places, allowing sufficient lead time for testing and correcting before the participants arrive and the items and equipment must be used.

Testing

Coordinators must watch with their own eyes and listen with their own ears to ensure that all equipment works. Coordinators must never leave the testing of equipment solely to the technicians or to anyone else. All equipment tests must be performed by the same technicians who will actually be operating the equipment during the event's agenda.

Not all technicians are open to evaluation and input from event coordinators. Only technicians who agree to allow the event coordinators to evaluate their work and suggest corrections should be hired. Technicians who will not cooperate and respond according to the desires and needs of the coordinators should never again be used or hired for any special event.

Instructing

Coordinators must be sure to explain program and equipment needs, personally, to each and every technician and expert who will be delivering or operating equipment during the event's agenda. It is essential that these individuals understand their responsibilities, the exact timing required, and the desired effects and results expected to accomplish the objectives for that particular portion of the event's agenda.

Supervising

Only experienced and expert technicians must be used for special events. In addition, at least one coordinator must be assigned to supervise each important portion of the event's agenda that requires sound, lighting, and other critical technical assistance to ensure quality and effective results.

The coordinator assigned to supervise a particular portion of the agenda must be an active participant in the testing of the equipment and in any rehearsals using the equipment. Moreover, he or she must stand beside the technicians and act as the producer during the time in which the equipment is being used, providing input for adjustments and changes as needed. This supervision is especially critical if an event is very important and has numerous VIPs in the audience.

Removing

Coordinators must ensure that items and equipment that have been used during the event and are no longer needed are removed from the event site as soon as possible after they are used so that they will be out of the way and will not be damaged or stolen.

Returning

As soon as possible after the items have been used or after the event has concluded, the coordinators must ensure that the items and equipment are returned undamaged to their proper places of origin.

Paying

Coordinators must arrange for prompt and proper payment of all bills related to the event's physical requirements.

Examples of Physical Requirements

There are as many physical requirements as are unique situations and meeting places; however, the following are among the more common ones:

1. Rooms and meeting spaces for each purpose
2. Furniture for each room, arranged according to plan
3. Seating plans
4. Seating charts
5. Name badges with large, easy-to-read lettering
6. Place cards
7. Table cards to help participants find their way to their assigned tables
8. Signs
9. Lecterns and podiums
10. Stages
11. Dance floors (permanent and portable)
12. Communications equipment
13. Audiovisual equipment, including sound, lighting, multimedia, and recording systems
14. Table covers and linens to match the event's color scheme
15. Displays
16. Booths
17. Participants' packets and souvenirs
18. Gifts for presenters and other VIPs, wrapped and identified with gift cards
19. Awards that have been engraved, marked, and arranged or displayed for presentation
20. Decorations

21. Centerpieces
22. Props
23. Rooms for changing clothes, resting, and refreshments for entertainers and presenters
24. Transportation vehicles
25. Storage space and cabinets to secure event supplies and participants' valuables
26. Printed materials, such as invitations, programs, and thank-you notes

Audiovisual Needs

Audiovisual equipment enables event participants to see and hear the agenda that has been planned for them by the event coordinators. It must be installed and operated by trained, highly skilled technicians who are knowledgeable about the exact type and model of equipment required by each program situation. Audiovisual technicians must also have the expertise to be able to operate, adjust, and repair the equipment properly, immediately, safely, and cooperatively, as required. After analyzing each segment of an event's program, expert technicians determine the exact audiovisual equipment that will meet the program's needs and create the desired effects.

Audiovisual equipment can be rented, leased (with or without a purchase option), or purchased. Decisions regarding how to acquire audiovisual equipment must be made from the standpoint of business (budget as well as taxes), practicality, and convenience. Regardless of whether the equipment is rented, leased, or purchased, it is wise to deal with only reputable dealers that will stand behind and service the equipment throughout its lifetime. State-of-the-art audiovisual equipment is expensive to own.

If an organization has an ongoing need to use particular equipment, however, and especially if the equipment can be used by more than one department within an organization, it is often more cost-effective and convenient to own the equipment and to maintain a knowledgeable staff of technicians.

Ownership

The pros of audiovisual equipment ownership are that (a) the equipment is available whenever it is needed, (b) it is convenient, (c) technicians are accustomed to operating the equipment that will be used so the quality of each program is guaranteed rather than having to rely on unknown equipment and the expertise of unknown technicians hired for an occasion,

(d) equipment costs can be depreciated, and (e) in the long run, money is saved by not having to continually rent equipment and hire technicians for each occasion.

Problems and considerations regarding equipment ownership are that (a) audiovisual equipment is expensive, fragile, and bulky; (b) storage must be convenient; (c) storage can be expensive if space must be rented or leased; (d) audiovisual equipment must be protected from theft and vandalism by proper security measures; (e) the equipment must be transported in special vehicles that may have to be rented, leased, or purchased with the equipment; (f) the organization must either have technicians on staff or have access to qualified, dependable, and competent technicians whenever needed; and (g) equipment becomes outdated and obsolete.

Examples of Equipment

Audio Equipment

- Amplifiers
- Mixers
- Speakers
- Microphones
- Signal processors
- Analog and digital cassette recorders
- Reel-to-reel tape recorders
- Disc players
- Intercom systems
- Podiums
- FM tuners
- Speaker stands
- Direct boxes
- Snakes
- Mic stands—straight, boom, table, or floor

Visual Equipment

- Video and data monitors—color
- Video and data projectors
- Computer interfaces
- Video players/recorders

- Editing components or packages
- Cameras
- Tripods
- Switchers
- Video lighting
- Timebase correctors
- Timecode generators/readers
- Video enhancers/switchers
- Video distribution amplifiers
- Waveform monitors/vectorscopes
- Modulators
- Transcoders
- Encoders
- Distribution amplifiers
- Switchers
- Batteries
- Battery chargers
- Battery belts
- Video production carts
- Video mate slide to video units
- 54-inch monitor carts with drapes

Visual or Multi-Image Equipment

- Slide projectors
- Motion picture projectors
- Overhead or opaque projectors
- Lenses
- Stackers
- Dissolve units
- Programmers
- Slide X-ray view boxes
- Data boosters
- Cassettes with sync
- Audio cassettes
- Electric pointers
- Laser pointers
- Flip charts with pads and pens

- Speaker timers
- Infrared slide projection wireless remotes
- Tensor lamps
- 54-inch carts with drapes
- Saf-lok stands
- Scaffolding
- Staging platforms
- Screens
- Screen dress kits
- Scenery
- Drapery

Lighting Equipment

- Follow spots
- Ellipsoidals
- Par floods
- Striplights and floods
- Dimmers
- Distribution equipment
- Stands or lifts
- Special effects
- Mirrorballs with motors
- Pinspots for mirrorballs
- Strobe lights with remotes
- Blacklights
- Fog machines
- Smoke machines
- Lasers

Module 9: Public Relations and Publicity

Public Relations

Public relations (PR) has been defined as making a planned effort to influence opinion through socially responsible and acceptable performance based on mutually satisfactory, two-way communication. Special events are ideal public relations vehicles because they address each part of this PR definition.

A Planned Effort

Each special event requires a significant amount of planned effort to be successful and accomplish its objectives.

To Influence Opinion

The opinions of a special event's participants and attendees, facilitators, and presenters are influenced by how these individuals experience the event. If the event is successful and accomplishes its objectives, those who have been involved will perceive their experiences as meaningful and worthy of their time, resulting in positive opinions about the event and its sponsors.

Through Socially Responsible and Acceptable Performance

Major goals of a special event are that (a) the event will be beneficial to everyone involved, (b) the event will accomplish its objectives, and (c) the event will be perceived as acceptable by those who attend it. It is desired that the event sponsors will be perceived as socially responsible and acceptable because of the time and resources they contributed to make the event possible. Many special events that have altruistic purposes or benefits, such as recognizing people and organizations that have made outstanding contributions to the community or raising money for nonprofit organizations such as United Way or the Special Olympics, are excellent examples of events that can be perceived as socially responsible and acceptable to the sponsor's public.

Based on Two-Way Communication

Well-planned special events use research, feedback, and input from an involved public. Ideas for improving future events and agendas can be obtained from quality event participant evaluation forms and conversations with key individuals who have been involved in the events and whose ideas and feedback provide valuable means of analysis and evaluation.

Publics

Publics can be defined as the individual people, groups of people, and organizations that an educational institution is trying to influence. Determining who a school's publics are, what they want from the school, and what the school wants from them is one of the most important first steps to take in public relations.

Publicity

Publicity can be defined as obtaining airtime and print space in various media as well as creating firsthand experiences to promote an idea or special event at no cost to the sponsoring organization. Editors provide free use of time and space because they believe the news value and special interest of a particular idea or event will be of interest to their audiences. Radio and television stations provide free time to nonprofit organizations and schools because the stations are mandated by their licensing agencies to provide specific amounts of public service information and airtime to their audiences.

Examples of External Publicity Tools

News Releases. News releases are brief news stories that are sent to targeted media editors and reporters with the hopes that the stories will be printed. News releases must include the "how, why, where, when, and what" about each story. News releases are written in journalistic style. They provide the name, title, and phone number of the contact person who can provide additional information and are often accompanied by photos with captions. News releases are frequently put onto wire services for immediate and vast distribution.

Public Service Spots. Public service spots are prepared for editors and reporters who represent radio and television stations. The spots include the same information as news releases except that the information is presented in a style and format that can be used on the air.

Press Conferences. Press conferences are called for very special news stories. Invitations are sent to editors of targeted media. Key senior administrators from schools and the district and often members of the board of education are used as spokespersons.

Press Kits. Press kits are special folders that include news releases, photos, and pertinent information about the stories and their sponsors. Press kits are distributed at press conferences and mailed to editors and reporters on request.

Publicity Stunts. Publicity stunts are exciting special events that have news or special interest value to the public. Publicity stunts often include important people doing important or very interesting things in interesting places. Exotic and unusual elements are created to arouse the curiosity of the media and, as a result, motivate them to send reporters to cover the events and then print stories in their publications or put the stories on the air.

Statement Stuffers. Some companies and private schools that send periodic bills and statements to their customers and parents include extra information in the same envelopes about issues of concern or interest to the company or school.

Examples of Internal PR Tools

Employee-Retiree Newspapers. Newspapers written for employees and retirees include news and information about the organization, its operations, and its special events.

Bulletin Boards. Organizations place bulletin boards in areas where employees and the general public gather. Information of interest to these people is posted on the boards.

Programs. Programs operated by schools can be used as publicity tools. An example of an internal program is an *employee assistance program.* An example of an external program is a *student community service volunteer program.* Special events are often a part of or related to these programs. Unique special events connected to very interesting programs build strong cases for media coverage.

Examples of Both
External and Internal PR Tools

Announcements. Announcements regarding a school's special event must be designed, written, printed, and distributed. It is essential that any information about the event be accurate and current in that your event represents your school and your district.

Printed Display Notices. Notices about special events can be printed and displayed on posters, table tents (messages and announcements printed on hard card stock that is folded in half and placed on tables where employees eat and relax), desktop fliers (paper that is placed on people's desks so the news will be seen as soon as the people arrive at work), signs, and banners. These printed notices can be displayed in areas where there is heavy traffic flow. Be sure to receive approvals from the site administrator before any posters or table tents are set up, and be sure to remove them immediately after the event.

Actions and Attitudes

People's actions and attitudes send messages to the people with whom they come in contact. Every effort must be made to ensure that representatives of schools and special events represent their organizations, the events, and themselves in the most professional, knowledgeable, helpful, and courteous manner possible.

Using PR Professionals

Many educational institutions, especially large ones, have formal public relations departments or use outside public relations agencies. These institutions prefer that all publicity be handled by those departments or agencies. Most PR departments and agencies insist on having total control over all contacts with external media and all information distributed to all of an organization's or a client's internal publics. The PR experts in these departments and agencies have years of PR training and experience. They would rather fit publicizing events into their busy schedules than risk the potentially damaging results of unprofessional contact with the media or of disorganized or confusing communication to internal publics.

Graphics

Graphics must be interesting, creative, and professional. Some graphics can be handled by using clip art (which can be purchased in artist supply, stationery, and bookstores). Layouts must be simple and easy to follow. Sophisticated and very special events should use the design talents of a professional designer.

Information to
Include in Your Publicity

Each promotional piece must contain the basic elements of journalism plus whatever information is necessary to be complete and answer the reader's questions.

Who

Examples of *who* questions include these: Who (what group of people) will be served by this event? Will we need to recruit any volunteers to help us facilitate the event? Are there any special restrictions, such as age? Are there any special requests for skills, expertise, and abilities, such as computer software, writing, graphics, construction? Will day care be provided for younger children and infants?

What

Examples of *what* questions include these: What is the name of the event, and what kind of an event is it? What kinds of activities will be involved? Will special training be required, and if so, what are the details?

An example of the *what* for a community service project is as follows:

The West Lake Special Olympics Regional Meet for special athletes: Volunteers are needed to help judge and time events and to serve as "huggers" as the athletes cross the finish lines; no special training is required.

An example of the *what* for a social activity is the following:

The Labor Day Weekend Potluck Picnic: Everyone is invited to celebrate our volunteer program's summer achievements and to welcome autumn.

When

An example of *when* questions include these: What are the day(s), month(s), date(s), (years) of the event? What is the exact time the event starts (for each specific date)? What is the exact time the event ends (for each specific date)? What are the starting and ending times of all shifts? What information do we need to know regarding travel time allowances, parking time allowances, and training time allowances?

Where (Include a Map)

Examples of *where* questions include these: What is the exact address, including street, area, city, county, and state (if necessary for out-of-state participants)? What are the very clear travel directions, including names of key freeways, off-ramps, highways, streets, and landmarks? What are the parking directions, including access streets, special parking spots, and parking validation information?

Why

Examples of *why* questions include these: Why is this event being held? What will be the benefits of the event to the school and any other sponsors? Why should people attend or volunteer to help?

How

An example of *how* questions include these: How is this event being handled by the school or district sponsor? Are there any special or unique details regarding the event about which the participants or volunteers must know before attending?

Any Additional Information

Examples of *additional information* questions include these: What are the benefits of participation for the school and any volunteers? Will the participants or volunteers receive any special promotional items or gifts?

RSVP Information

An example of an *RSVP information* question includes, To whom should the RSVP and sign-up forms be sent? Be sure to include that person's name, title, complete external address, internal address, daytime phone number with area code, and evening or weekend phone number with area code, if necessary.

Registration Information

Include a sign-up or registration form that includes the following information:

- First and last name of the registrants
- Daytime phone number with area code
- Evening and weekend phone numbers with area code
- Home address, including street, city, state, and zip code
- Number and names of any guests who will also be participating
- Specific requests for special volunteer assignments
- Arrival time
- Number of hours of service committed
- T-shirt needs and sizes

Approvals

Because people will be making decisions, forming opinions, and following instructions based on the information they receive about your event, all publicity produced for the event must receive approval prior to being released. Failure to follow this procedure can result in embarrassment, liability, confusion, and occasionally accidents and anger.

Each and every promotional piece you prepare for your event must be reviewed and approved by the key administrators responsible for the event before it is sent to anyone or posted in a public place. Each oral and written publicity piece must be submitted for approval using an approval form, such as the sample Publicity Approval Form found in Appendix B. The approval form and corresponding publicity item are first submitted to the key event administrator, who will determine if any further approval is required.

Timing

All elements of public relations regarding a special event must be strategized well early in the planning stages of the event. It is essential that the people who handle the publicity for a special event schedule release dates that will coincide with the deadlines of the targeted external and internal media.

When the event is a community service project involving the recruitment and use of volunteers, it is essential that the fliers and announcements regarding the event be distributed or mailed according to a prescribed schedule to allow sufficient time for the volunteers to register and send in their sign-up forms. Also, occasionally the community organization that will be served requires advance notice of the numbers and names of your volunteers for the organization to do its planning and make necessary security and special arrangements.

Distribution or Mailing

The lead event coordinator is responsible for assembling and distributing or mailing all announcements for the event. The key administrator of the event may be able to provide preaddressed labels for all of the invitees and volunteers for the event. You may want to recruit some of your volunteer friends to help you assemble, stuff, and affix the labels and postage to the envelopes or fliers. A video movie party is often a great way to take care of this task. If postage is required, ask the key administrator of the event to provide the postage or an appropriate method of payment.

RSVPs

RSVPs to general events and responses and sign-up forms for volunteers to participate in community service events should be sent to the lead event coordinator unless another decision is made that is more suitable to the situation and is agreeable to the key administrator. A common alternative is to have the RSVPs and sign-up forms be returned directly to the key event administrator.

Module 10: Security, Liability, and Permits

No Assumptions

The lesson to be learned from this module is simple: In matters regarding security, liability, and permits, you must make no assumptions about anything! The results of poor special event related decisions that cause security, liability, or permit problems can be hazardous to the health of a school, the administrator of the department overseeing the event, and the overall event coordinator. Many of these problems are caused by faulty assumptions.

Faulty Assumption 1—History

Statement: They did it that way last time, so I am sure it is OK to do it that way again.

Warning: Just because they did it that way last time does not mean they were doing the right thing or doing the thing right. It just means that nothing went wrong or that they did not get caught. If something does go wrong this time that results in a big problem while you are in charge, you could be in trouble. Besides, things could have changed since they did the event last time.

Faulty Assumption 2—Perceived Importance

Statement: There are so many things that need to be done, and this one is not worth the time to check it out.

Warning: Every special event has thousands of details that must be done. Anything that has to do with security, liability, or permits is worth the time to check out. If you do not, someone could be injured; something could be stolen or damaged; the event could be stopped anywhere in the process from design to implementation by a higher authority; or a person or an organization, including yours, could become part of a lawsuit. Any or all of these things could happen just because an individual coordinating the event did not think the issue was worth the time to investigate.

Faulty Assumption 3—Responsibility

Statement: I am not in charge. If my boss is not worried about this, then I am not going to worry about it.

Warning: It is your responsibility to do a competent job by producing a successful special event. It is also your job to make your boss look good. Your boss may not know that something is important because he or she is not an expert in special events.

If you know that something is important and must be investigated, then you must investigate it or do a good, strong job of explaining to your boss about the importance of the issue, receiving permission to conduct the investigation, following through, and then informing your boss, in writing, of the results. You must put forth this effort for his or her protection and information as well as for your own.

Scapegoats

If your boss forbids you to conduct the investigation, then you must protect yourself by writing a memo to him or her that discusses the topic and verifies that he or she instructed you not to investigate the issue. When things go wrong, some bosses look for scapegoats. If you have been conscientious and thorough in handling your event responsibilities and you have protected yourself, there is a good chance your boss will have to look elsewhere for a scapegoat if a security, liability, or permit problem occurs.

Faulty Assumption 4—Ignorance

Statement: I have never heard of this before. This sounds silly. It cannot be right, and it is a total waste of time. I am not going to bother with it.

Warning: Each person must realize that he or she does not and cannot know everything about anything. A little humility is an important and desirable character trait for a coordinator of special events. In that most coordinators are not attorneys or city officials, there are probably thousands of things event coordinators do not know about security, liability, and permits—things that could have a strong, negative impact on special events. Ignorance is no excuse for anyone to make a careless mistake, especially coordinators of special events.

Faulty Assumption 5—Disagreement

Statement: This is just a lot of red tape. I am not going to jump through these hoops.

Warning: An event coordinator's job is not to agree or disagree with laws, rules, and regulations that can impact a special event. His or her job is to plan and implement special events and to protect their school and district in the most professional manner possible, which includes ensuring that events conform to the laws, rules, and regulations that pertain to them.

Security Issues

Security issues are critical to the success of an event. It is the event coordinator's responsibility to make sure that he or she has "secured" every asset, including the school's and district's reputation and every person who will be attending the event to the greatest degree possible prior to the beginning of the event. A spectacularly successful event can be spoiled in the administration's eyes by the loss of or damage to one valuable piece of school property or the injury of anyone involved in the event.

Several examples of security issues include the following:

- The protection of valuable school equipment
- The protection of participants' valuables and personal items
- The protection of VIPs
- Politically sensitive issues that draw emotional or hostile participants to an event
- Picketing
- Demonstrations
- Using a potentially hazardous community site for an event
- Using dangerous or secluded parking areas
- Gang activity
- Transporting people and equipment to and from the event
- Firearms
- Bomb threats

Security Resources

School districts and schools have many resources that can be called on to help event coordinators ensure that their events are as secure as possible. The following are some examples of security resources:

- An internal security department that provides counsel, guards, and police
- External security companies that provide counsel and guards
- Personal escorts to parked cars, especially after dark
- Storage areas and cabinets with secure locks to store valuable equipment and personal possessions when they are not being used
- Safe deposit boxes

- Bodyguards
- Electronic surveillance equipment
- Electronic search equipment
- Alarm systems
- Communications equipment
- A thorough, well-researched security plan that is custom designed for an event and approved by the administrator of the department overseeing the event

Liability Issues

The following are the major things that create liability issues:

- Damage
- Injury
- Libel
- Breach of confidentiality
- Negligence

If any aspect of planning the event creates one of these types of problems, the event coordinator must resolve the problem. Liability problems can be prevented up to a point, but then "Murphy" and fate take over. For events that will naturally incur a larger than average amount of risk, it may be advisable for the school or district to purchase an insurance rider to cover the event. The district's insurance department can suggest the necessary steps to take in this regard.

Liability Resources

Coordinators of special events must not operate alone whenever liability issues and problems arise. Doing so will only aggravate a problem and the potential degree of risk and responsibility. Use of any one or a combination of the following experts is advised either before or after an event involving potential liability or resulting in actual liability problems:

- The district's risk management or insurance department
- Internal attorneys
- External attorneys

- Insurance agents
- Public relations practitioners

Permits

Because school events occur in public places and involve various sizes of community groups, permits are often part of the routine planning necessary for school events. Each and every city's laws differ regarding permits. The best assumption to make regarding permits is to assume that you will probably need to get one. Then you can begin doing some healthy detective work to find your way to the correct and proper district department and city department that will give you the right advice regarding permits. Validate the advice you receive and then follow it. Be sure to allow plenty of lead time to get the approvals and make the arrangements that are necessary so that your event will not be negatively impacted by not having a permit.

The following are pertinent permit issues:

- Defining and understanding the meaning of a "public place"
- Holding public meetings and events in public places
- Maximum occupancy regulations
- Safety
- Evacuation regulations and procedures
- Fires
- Emergencies
- Disasters
- Plans for emergencies and disasters

Permit Resources

The following are some permit resources:

- The district office that handles permit issues
- The landlord
- The office of the building
- The fire marshall
- The police or sheriff's department
- City, county, state, and federal public authorities

State and School Board
Education Codes and Policies

During the preapproval phase of planning a school special event, the event coordinator should check with the top school administrator or the appropriate district representative to ensure that the proposed event does not violate any aspect of the state education code or the school board policies.

Module 11: Transportation

Getting There

When it comes to special events, getting there is half the battle. People are far more likely to enjoy and appreciate their experience at a special event if they are in no way inconvenienced or distressed from the time they leave their homes or offices until the time they have arrived safely at the site and have walked through the entrance enthusiastic and eager to participate.

Coordination

Due to the importance of transportation to the success of an event, it is strongly recommended that all transportation arrangements be handled by a single event coordinator who will work directly with all transportation agents and companies.

The individual assigned to coordinate the travel for an event must possess patience, excellent people skills, and strong negotiation skills. He or she must have the ability to handle many complex tasks simultaneously and to manage details accurately and completely.

While making travel arrangements, many details and loose ends can be overlooked, misplaced, or forgotten. As a result, feelings of fear, frustration, and anxiety are experienced by the travel coordinator, who must deal with dissatisfied participants' stress, anger, and hostility when their travel plans have been changed or thwarted. Appointing a highly qualified, conscientious person to coordinate the transportation for a special event greatly decreases the chances of important details falling through the cracks.

Simple Arrangements

An example of simple travel arrangements is when the location of an event is in a community in which the participants live or work and one with which they are familiar. They provide their own transportation to and from the event using the method with which they are normally accustomed during their daily routines.

Even though an event is held in a familiar location, the travel coordinator must approach the arrangements from the point of view that the participants do not know where to go or how to get there. Helpful information must be provided to the participants in their invitations or confirmation materials.

Directions

Travel directions must be clearly written and include the names and numbers of the freeways and major streets that must be used. Enclosing a clearly drawn map with arrows pointing to the event site is strongly recommended.

Parking

Instructions must include street entrances to designated parking lots and structures; instructions for locating designated event parking spots within lots or structures; and information about parking costs, including maximum charges, acceptable methods of payment, and instructions for obtaining reimbursements or validations. If the sponsor of an event is covering the parking costs, enclosing a parking pass is strongly recommended.

Complex Arrangements

Events that are located in cities to which participants must travel long distances require special, more complex arrangements. Major travel arrangements involving many participants usually require legal contracts between the sponsors and the service providers. All contracts must be carefully reviewed by the administrator of the department overseeing the event prior to being signed by the individual designated by that administrator to sign on behalf of the organization.

Airline Arrangements

Instructions for how to travel from the host city's airport to the event site or the selected hotel must be included in the participants' invitations or confirmation materials. In addition, the travel coordinator must be available to respond to calls from participants who wish to clarify how they will be traveling from the airport to the event site.

Sometimes an event sponsor makes special arrangements with a specific airline to designate and advertise that airline as the "official event airline." In return, the airline offers specially reduced rates to event participants. All arrangements and negotiations relative to such an agreement must be managed by the event's designated travel coordinator. Information about this type of added benefit for participants must be clearly explained in the event's announcements and confirmation materials.

Reservation Service

Some event sponsors provide airline reservation service through a designated travel agency or travel department. Services include helping participants select convenient flights, processing payments, and printing and delivering tickets. Some event sponsors provide airline reservation service through a designated event travel coordinator, who in turn uses a designated travel agency or travel department.

Tickets

If all travel arrangements are being handled by one travel coordinator, there are two options for ticket delivery: The airline or travel agency could deliver the tickets directly to the participants, or they could deliver them to the travel coordinator for the event. The latter method is recommended in that the event coordinator can ensure that all ticketing and reservations have been handled correctly prior to sending the tickets to the participants. This extra precaution reduces the opportunity for error.

Covered Travel Costs

If the event is covering the travel costs for its participants, the travel agency or designated travel coordinator handles all reservations for the participants as discussed previously and then bills the ticket costs to the proper organization's designated budget code.

Other Travel Arrangements

Other kinds of complex travel arrangements must be made through reputable companies. When possible, it is best to select companies that have provided satisfactory, quality service to one or more of the event's sponsors. Examples of other travel arrangements required by special events include the following:

- Car rentals
- Shuttle buses
- Chartered buses
- Limousines
- Helicopters (flight schedules for the helicopters and passengers and authorized landing sites must be arranged)
- Available citywide transportation, such as taxis, limousines, subways, and buses
- Trains
- Boats
- Ferries
- Cruise ships

Module 12: Accommodations

Creature Comforts

Special events create a reason for people to have to leave their homes and offices—places with which they are accustomed—and go to new and often strange places. When they arrive and during their stay at an event, people want to feel comfortable and at ease. The selection of an event site is very important. A great site will set the stage for an exciting and new experience throughout a special event. A poor site will create discomfort and take away from the effects and effectiveness of an event, making it less than special. For example, a spectacular agenda will be overshadowed by sleeping rooms that are too small, faulty plumbing, uncomfortable temperatures, and disturbances caused by remodeling and repairs of the facility during the event.

Cause for Second Thoughts

If participants are uncomfortable within their surroundings during the event, they will wonder if perhaps they could have done something better with their time and resources, such as staying at the office and finishing some work or staying at home and being with their families.

Abe Lincoln was right; although "you can't please all of the people all of the time," in the case of special events, you must try. Striving to please requires careful and expert analysis of potential event sites, matching potential sites with the backgrounds and expectations of the people who will attend the event, making the best possible decision about the event's location and facility, and being willing and able to accept criticism and solve problems when someone is not pleased with some aspect of the event's location and its accommodations.

It Pays to Go Out of Your Way

If you go out of your way to be responsive, to solve problems promptly, to be sincerely committed to ensuring the comfort of each participant, and to do all of this with a smile, then you have done all that anyone can expect of you.

Site Considerations

The following are 26 site considerations to help you make a good decision about the accommodations for your event:

1. Location—city and facility
2. Season and weather conditions
3. Convenience
4. Available and inexpensive ground and air transportation; convenient service to and from airports
5. Type of site (e.g., hotel, convention center, training room, or university campus)
6. Age, condition, style, and decor

7. Accommodations for handicapped participants throughout the facility

8. Remodeling or repairs during event

9. Cost of rooms, food, beverages, and other services

10. Availability of on-site support services (e.g., office, copying, phones, secretarial, fax, audiovisual, and food service)

11. Adaptable meeting rooms, varying in size and arrangement possibilities

12. Sleeping accommodations (e.g., the size, decor, special amenities, and cleanliness of the rooms)

13. Location of restaurants and dining rooms or availability of room service

14. Quality of food and beverages

15. Safety

16. Proximity to shopping and entertainment

17. Type and convenience of available extracurricular activities

18. Quality, quantity, and professionalism of on-site staff assigned to the event

19. Availability and lead time required for reservations

20. Amount of down payment required

21. Refund policy

22. Security

23. Ownership of the site and the affiliations of the owners

24. Restrictive rules and regulations

25. Availability of no-smoking rooms and areas

26. Convenient and fast check-in/check-out service

7

Community Service
and Volunteer Projects

The Important Difference

There is one important difference between a community service project and any other type of special event: *the volunteers.* Coordinators of community service projects must apply all of the other aspects of good special event management discussed in this book *and* know how to deal with and treat volunteers.

Volunteers are special people. They volunteer because they want to help, not because they have to help or because they are being paid to do a job. Consequently, it is essential that throughout a volunteer event all event coordinators treat the volunteers with the utmost respect, patience, and gratitude, no matter how stressful the event becomes. If volunteers feel good about the event and feel appreciated and valued, they will volunteer again and again.

Research the Project

The first step in coordinating a community service project is to conduct research about the project and volunteer service to be provided. The history of the project and important basic facts will come from several sources.

Project Proposal Form

Community service projects begin with the completion of the Community Service Project Proposal Form (see Appendix C), including all necessary approvals. This form should be completed by the lead event coordinator or a designee. The information given on this form will tell you what you need to know about the project in general and will provide the names of contact people who can furnish you with any additional information you will require to do your job.

The Agency or School to Be Served

The person(s) listed on the form as the contact(s) should be called, interviewed, and, preferably, visited. The goal is to learn exactly what service is required by the agency or school from the people who will volunteer for this event. This information will enable you to advise the volunteers properly and correctly, and it will enable you to perform your role knowledgeably and capably.

Previous Project Files and Records

If this project or similar events have been conducted previously by your school, request a copy of those project files, reports, and records. It will also be useful to see if there is any history of your school working with the project's community organization(s). These files and records will enable you to feel more confident and to do a better job as the project coordinator.

The Key Contact From the Community Organization or School

The following steps should be taken when you are ready to introduce yourself to the community organization or school:

1. Call the key contact from the organization or school.

2. Make an appointment to visit the organization and receive a tour so that you can learn about the organization, its purpose, and its needs.

3. If possible, meet the chief executive or principal.

4. Present yourself as a representative of your school and explain your role in the project.

5. Discover how your school and its volunteers can be of service for this particular community service project or during an ongoing relationship.

6. Make sure you know and understand the exact nature of the service your volunteers will be asked to provide.

7. If you have a question about whether your school's volunteers will be able to or should perform the exact service requested by the community organization, check with the appropriate administrator from your school.

8. Establish a positive working relationship with the key contact from the organization.

9. Demonstrate your personal interest in and concern for the organization and its purpose.

10. Do everything you can to send only volunteers who are capable and desirable of performing the exact services required by the organization.

11. Find out how much advanced notice is required by the organization to know the number and names of the people who will volunteer.

12. Find out if the organization will provide food or refreshments for your volunteers or if they must bring or provide their own food.

The Management at the Project Site

The following steps should be taken when your project is going to occur at a site that is different from the site where the community organization or school is located:

1. Call the key contact, manager, or administrator from the project site. Examples of possible sites include a school, nonprofit organization, city park, amusement park, restaurant, hotel, or private residence.

2. Make an appointment to visit the site, meet the key contact, and receive a tour so that you can see the site and understand the amount of space, logistics, and resources that will be available for your project.

3. Determine what resources will be available at the site. Examples include the amount, location, and cost of parking spots; the communications equipment; the eating facilities; the tables and chairs; the dishes and utensils; the kitchen facilities; the services for children; the rest rooms; the swimming pool; the recreation space; the sports equipment; and the handicap access.

4. Present yourself as a representative of your school.

5. Discover any restrictions that will apply to your volunteers. Examples include restrictions on the age of children who can attend, closing time, dress code, and noise level requirements.

6. Establish a positive working relationship with the key contact from the project site.

7. Do everything you can to ensure that the participants from your school respect and care for the project site, its resources, and its personnel.

8. Get a confirmation in writing of any costs, including tips and any extras, and include these expenses in your budget.

Prepare the Budget

Some volunteer service projects will not incur any costs for your school, and it is common that many cost-related items will be provided by the organization you will be serving. If costs are likely to be incurred, however, review Chapter 4. Then prepare a budget in an appropriate format for your school. Be sure to have the budget approved by all necessary people before you proceed with your project.

Plan the Project

To help plan your project, a good place to begin would be a review of the discussion about planning provided in Chapter 5 and the planning checklist provided in Appendix A. In addition to these, be sure to use the Community Service Project Planning Checklist provided in Appendix C to help prepare for your project.

Recruit the Volunteers

Fliers and Other Promotional Items

Your project will be publicized primarily through the fliers and other communication pieces that you produce. You will find ideas and guidance you will need to promote your project and recruit your volunteers by reading Module 3 found in Chapter 6. People who sign up for your event will return a coupon either to you or an appropriate person designated by one of your school administrators.

Word of Mouth

You may also wish to make some oral announcements at group activities and events to recruit people for your project. In addition, you should "talk up" your project whenever possible.

Processing Responses

Each person who signs up for your project by completing and returning a volunteer sign-up coupon, including, if applicable, the names of his or her guests, should be registered on the Community Service Project Volunteer Sign-Up Form provided in Appendix C. Attach each registration coupon to your sign-up form and keep these items together in a file folder for quick reference throughout the phases of your project. You will use the form as a reference to send confirmations and other communications to each person who volunteers to participate in your project.

Confirmations

When you receive each sign-up coupon, send the volunteer or participant a confirmation package that includes the following:

- A note or letter thanking him or her for volunteering
- Specific instructions about what to do, where to go, when to arrive, where to park, where to meet, what to wear, what to bring, what not to bring, what will be involved, any restrictions or limitations, and any special needs

- A map
- Your daytime and evening or weekend phone number (or your designee's) in case someone must cancel or needs additional information
- *Important—for emergencies:* The phone number with area code of the community organization as well as the phone number at the project location during the time the volunteers will be there

If you have carefully followed all of the recommendations and accomplished the items on your checklists leading up to the community service project, then you and your volunteers will be ready for the project on D-Day.

Signing In and Out

The general operational tasks required on D-Day as well as the wrap-up tasks are explained in the next two chapters. These routine tasks and steps are to be completed whether or not the event uses volunteers. When you coordinate a project that uses your school's volunteers, however, you must also obtain and record (a) the number of volunteers, (b) the names of the volunteers who participate, and (c) their hours of service. It is essential that your school, district, and the volunteers receive appropriate credit for the community service provided through the project. That "credit" is determined by meticulously logging information about the volunteers and their hours of service.

You must be sure to provide a separate volunteer registration or sign-in table and one or two chairs for the volunteers or your assistants who will coordinate the table. This table must be placed at a clearly visible location near the entrance to the project at least 1 hour prior to the arrival time of your school's volunteers.

Be sure to put a sign on the table so that the volunteers will see the table immediately when they arrive. Each volunteer and his or her guests, if any, must *sign in* when they arrive at the project and *sign out* when they leave (see Community Service Project Sign-In and Sign-Out Form in Appendix C). Their hours of service must be recorded on the Community Service Project Summary Report Form (see Appendix C).

Completing the Service Report

At the conclusion of the community service project, the lead coordinator should collect all sign-in and sign-out forms, tally up the number of volunteers and hours of service, and record this important information on the project summary report form.

Copies of this summary report should be given to your school's principal and any other key people who are involved or interested in the project. If more than one community service project is performed during a school year, someone should produce a summary report for the school year by combining all of the information from each summary report and recording it on a separate summary *Annual Report.*

This kind of information is invaluable for public relations and community relations for your school. School and district administrators as well as school board members will be very pleased to see the reports and discover the important impact your school and its volunteers have made on their community.

8

D-Day
What to Do During the Event

Sole or Joint Coordination

If your school is participating in an event that is cosponsored or co-coordinated, you may be assigned general coordination responsibilities during the overall event; in addition, you will have specific coordination responsibilities for the participants and volunteers who will be arriving from your school. The information presented in this chapter will apply to *each* type of coordination responsibilities you may have. That is, you must ensure that all participants and volunteers from your school are informed about what they must do so that they will be well organized and make a positive contribution to the overall event. *And* you must perform the general coordination tasks assigned to you to ensure that the overall event is a success. As you read the information in this chapter, be sure to apply it to *each* of these two coordination situations.

Arrival of the Lead
Event Coordinator

There are four important reasons why the lead event coordinator (you) should arrive at least 1 hour earlier than any of the volunteers or participants from your school:

1. So that you can "settle in" and set up the sign-in/sign-out or registration table and other supplies for your school's participants and volunteers
2. To put up any directional signs that will help your school's volunteers and participants find their way to the parking area, entrance, and registration table
3. So that you can greet those who arrive early
4. To check in with the coordinators from the community organization that will be served to let them know you are there and that other participants and volunteers will be arriving soon and to give the organization's coordinators boosts of confidence and reassurance

Assigning Tasks and Activities

People given coordination or supervision assignments during the event should receive the assignments well in advance of the event so that they will know exactly what is expected and exactly when they should start and finish. Assignments should be made graciously and with appreciation and enthusiasm to build team spirit.

The Importance of Flexibility

It is not always possible to know exactly what must be done when the event begins. Often it is a matter of determining what needs to be done at the time and then filling in as needed. Try to prepare your volunteers and assistants for the need to be flexible; they may have been told they would be doing certain tasks prior to the event, but things may change.

Types of Assignments

The following are examples of types of coordination and supervision assignments that can be made:

- Directing traffic and parking
- Registration (sign-in and sign-out)
- Crowd control
- Communication (walkie-talkies or runners)
- Assigning volunteers to specific tasks
- Making sure everyone has whatever is needed to do a good job
- Answering questions
- Food or refreshment set-up and service
- Serving as the photographer
- Troubleshooting
- Child care
- "Guard" of volunteers' and participants' valuables, such as purses and jackets

Registration

There are two kinds of registration: (a) the registration of the volunteers and participants from your school who will be providing service and support to the sponsoring organization's event and (b) the registration of overall participants of the event as they arrive. In certain situations, these two groups may be one and the same.

The registration of your school's volunteers and participants is an essential and extremely important part of the process, as explained in Chapter 7. Each and every one of your school's volunteers and participants must sign in and sign out at the event using a registration form or list of participants developed for the purpose (such as in Appendix C).

The registration table for your school's participants and volunteers must be at an easily seen and easily accessible location, right at the entrance to the event. The table must be staffed at all times throughout the event by one or preferably two people from your school. This table is *in addition to* the primary registration table for the community organization's event, which also must be set up at the entrance and staffed throughout the event.

Supervision of Volunteers and Assistants

Your school's volunteers and your coordinating assistants require supervision during events for the following reasons:

- To ensure that the volunteers and assistants represent your school appropriately and well
- To ensure that the volunteers' behavior is appropriate and in accordance with the event's goals and standards
- To ensure that the volunteers and event coordinators provide the service that has been requested by the community organization
- To provide assistance to your volunteers and assistants who need help
- To ensure that the volunteers and assistants are safe
- To be aware of problems that occur and to provide assistance in their solutions
- To ensure that volunteers and assistants enjoy themselves while participating in the event
- To ensure that the volunteers feel needed and useful

Supervision of volunteers and coordinating assistants must be performed with the utmost professionalism, courtesy, kindness, empathy, friendliness, helpfulness, and patience.

Solving Problems

Problems that occur before, during, or after an event must be solved immediately, professionally, tactfully, correctly, and in a manner that brings about a resolution that is mutually satisfactory to each party, if possible. Serious problems, especially those affecting the relationship of your school with the community organization being served or those resulting in potential liability for the sponsor or your school, must be immediately reported to the appropriate people, including the most appropriate administrator of your school.

It may be necessary for experts representing the sponsoring organization and your school or district to become involved in the resolution of a difficult problem to resolve it satisfactorily for all parties. In difficult problem situations, you will feel more confident if you know that you are not alone and that you will be helped whenever you need assistance by experts.

Expectations Versus Results

In a special event, your expectations are that (a) everyone will perform, (b) all details will be handled, (c) everyone's needs will be fulfilled, and (d) all objectives will be accomplished *as planned and without a flaw*. Any differences between the expectations of the event and the actual results, both positive and negative, must be noted in writing, discussed, and analyzed during the debriefing meeting, which will be discussed in the next chapter.

Giving Thanks

All people need to be thanked for their service, but volunteers especially need to be thanked. Because you are the event coordinator, it is essential that you demonstrate and extend the gratitude and appreciation of your school as well as your own to each and every volunteer, assistant, and participant who worked in your event. During the event, thanks should be expressed verbally; physically, with a handshake, a smile, or a pat on the back; with sincerity; and with enthusiasm. Other people who should extend thanks are your assistants, the volunteers assigned to staff the registration table, and anyone you have assigned to supervise any aspect of the event.

Appreciation should be shared as the volunteers and participants arrive and sign in, by saying something such as, "Thanks for coming! We're really glad you are here with us today! We need you!" Each volunteer should be thanked during the day, at least once, by saying something similar to, "How's it going? Thanks again!" And people should be thanked as they sign out and leave, by saying something such as, "Thanks again! You did a great job. Hope you had a good time. See you again soon!"

Departure of the Lead Event Coordinator

You should be the last person from your school to leave your special event or community service project. If you cannot stay until the end, then appoint a responsible person to handle the final details. Before you or your designee leaves, you will need to do the following four things:

1. Do a last minute "sweep" of the area and make sure nothing has been left behind. If you find something that belongs to one of your

volunteers or participants, take it with you so that you can help put it back into his or her hands as soon as possible.

2. Say good-bye and thank you to the coordinators of the event who represent the community organization you served, asking if they need any more help before you leave.

3. Say good-bye to the event site manager.

4. Ensure that everyone has safely left the event site before you leave. If you discover anyone who is having problems such as car trouble, stay with him or her until the problem is solved and the person is safe, secure, and gone.

9

Wrapping Up With a Flair

It Ain't Over 'Til It's Over

Throughout most special events, people make requests, things occur that were not planned and that require resolution, and social graces must be performed. Because so many details and items are demanding time and attention during the event, many of these items must be handled after the event is officially over. It is essential to follow up on all of these concluding details immediately after the conclusion of the event. Prompt follow-up will ensure that the effort put forth to demonstrate professionalism and to deliver a sterling event will not be tarnished by slow or no follow-up and poor manners.

Coordination Details

The lead event coordinator must oversee and ensure the completion of the follow-up items. The event coordinators responsible for the particular pieces of the agenda or event plan that require the need for follow-up must be responsible for the fulfillment of the resulting follow-up items. Examples of these items include the following:

1. Follow up on any requests made by any administrator from your school or by a representative of senior management from the community organization served.

2. Send thank-you notes and letters to anyone who participated in the event's program and contributed to its success (sponsors, speakers, entertainers, suppliers, vendors, and contributors), ensuring that they are signed by the most appropriate person.

3. Pay any person or organization that performed a service for a fee.

4. Present or send thank-you gifts and cards to all volunteers who participated in the coordination of the event.

5. Present or send thank-you gifts and cards to all staff members outside of the department that was responsible for overseeing the event, who were not paid out of that department's budget. (Although those staff members did receive payment for their services, they should be treated with extra special consideration and appreciation for political and practical reasons.)

6. Return equipment and supplies rented or borrowed for the event.

7. Take down all decorations and signs and distribute them appropriately.

8. Make sure that no items belonging to your school or the event sponsor(s), if applicable, or anyone connected with the event are left behind.

9. Send awards and materials to scheduled participants who were unable to attend.

10. Transport materials and supplies back to the office or their proper final destinations.

11. Negotiate contracts related to the next event regarding issues such as use of the same hotel or conference center.

12. Arrange for permits for the next event.

13. Make reservations for sites and services for the next event, including down payments when required.

14. Send copies of materials to people who requested them.

15. Answer questions that required further research to provide a correct answer.

16. Resolve problems that occurred prior to or during the event.

17. Handle complaints that were received during the event.

18. Deliver complaints in the most appropriate, effective, and professional manner regarding any substandard service provided by any person or organization prior to, during, or following the event.

19. Recruit coordinators (including staff, consultants, and volunteers) for the next event.

20. Return personal items to participants who forgot them.

21. Thank co-coordinators for their help and extend appreciation for their participation on the event team.

22. Follow up on all public relations efforts to see if any press releases, public service spots, or other PR efforts successfully resulted in media coverage.

23. Distribute positive press clippings and information about the event to appropriate representatives of your school's administration, if appropriate, and to the appropriate representatives of senior management from other event sponsors, if applicable and appropriate.

24. Review the event checklist prior to attending the debriefing meeting.

25. Make personal notes about how you feel the event went, paying special attention to areas in which you felt you could have done a better job or problems you encountered that you wish you would have handled in a different manner. (These notes are for your own personal use and development and need not be shown to anyone else, although they may prove helpful in your participation in the debriefing session.)

26. Reward yourself with something you really want for your hard work regarding the event.

Debriefing

A *debriefing meeting* can be defined as a meeting of all of the key special event coordinators and supervisors who were involved in producing a special event; the purpose of the meeting is to obtain everyone's input regarding their experiences, observations, and opinions during the preparation, implementation, and follow-up of the event to properly and objectively evaluate the success of the event. Debriefing meetings must be held as soon as possible after the formal conclusion of the event.

Some Guiding Questions

The following questions will help you and those who will attend the debriefing meeting to gain the most from the evaluation process.

- What questions can be asked that will enable all of those who must attend the debriefing meeting to understand and evaluate the degree of success for the overall event and each of its specific parts?
- Were the sponsors satisfied with the results of the event? Why or why not?
- Did the event accomplish its goals and objectives? Why or why not?
- What were the event's strengths?
- What were the event's weaknesses?
- How much did the event cost, and did the event stay within its budget? If the event went over budget, why and in what areas?
- If this event was previously produced and especially if our organization was involved as a sponsor, how does the current evaluation of the event compare with the previous events?
- How was the event successful? (Define *success*.)
- Regarding community service projects, was the community organization satisfied with our help?
- Did everyone enjoy themselves?
- Were there any problems?
- How were the problems handled?
- How could this event have been more successful?
- Do we think this event should be repeated?
- Were there any outstanding coordinators and volunteers who could be used for future events?

Evaluation by
Event Coordinators

To determine the overall success of the event, event coordinators can ask themselves, "Did each element of our event accomplish its goals and objectives? If not, why not? What problems developed and why? How can these problems be prevented in the future?" Each of the following major pieces of the event should be evaluated to help the event coordinators determine the overall success of the event:

- Checklist
- Time line
- Attendees
- Announcements
- Agenda
- Ambiance
- Accommodations
- Meals
- Transportation
- Arrivals
- Departures
- Public relations
- Physical requirements
- Audiovisual needs
- Communication systems
- Security
- Liability
- Permits
- D-Day

Evaluation by Event Participants

If the participants and key individuals were asked to return event evaluation forms by mail, several weeks can pass before the forms are received and they can be evaluated. It is, therefore, preferred to collect the evaluation forms before the people leave each session or the overall event. The event coordinators may wish to devise clever ways to "bribe" the people into completing and turning in the evaluation forms.

Timing of Debriefing Meetings

It may be necessary to conduct two debriefing meetings. It is important that the first debriefing meeting be held immediately after the conclusion of the event. The results of the first meeting must be put into writing, ensuring that the written notes accurately reflect the feelings, opinions, and ideas expressed during that meeting. A second debriefing meeting must then be set after the participant evaluation forms have been received and evaluated. During the second debriefing meeting, the new information must be analyzed independently and then combined with the information from the first meeting to make one final, comprehensive event evaluation report.

Written Event Evaluations

Depending on the type of event, a special event can be evaluated and measured. A sample Event Evaluation Form is included in Appendix D. You can use this form as it stands or let the questions on the form generate ideas for you to develop your own evaluation form for your event. If the event is a community service project, it should be evaluated by using the Community Service Project Summary Report Form (Appendix C). All evaluation forms must be completed immediately after the event has concluded.

The debriefing report (or evaluation form) does not require approval, beyond the agreement of those who produce it, that its contents are correct and accurately reflect their opinions and evaluations of the event. The report's contents, however, must be shared with the administrator of the department responsible for the event, and he or she must decide if anyone else within or outside of your school should review it.

Giving Thanks

Although you gave thanks during the event, there will probably be some extra special people you should thank before you put the event behind you. Examples of the people who should receive additional thanks include the following:

- Any representatives from your school and district, such as members of the school board or top administrators, who attended or who provided assistance to you and your event in any way
- Your assistants, if you had any
- Any key volunteers or participants whose help was invaluable to you and who really helped to make the event a success

Personalized thank-you notes or letters are always a good way to express your appreciation. In addition, you may want to give extra special people some tangible symbols of your appreciation. The administrator of your school who was responsible for the event may be able to provide you with some ideas (and financial assistance) for thank-you gifts or even some promotional items that will help you to express your appreciation.

Thank-you notes, letters, and gifts should be sent or given soon after the event while it is still fresh in everyone's mind. If you wait too long to send them, they will lose their effect and say something negative about your organizational skills, follow through, and sincerity.

10

Reward Yourself
Author's Epilogue

As a public relations practitioner, I have managed numerous special events. None has compared with the experience of producing and premiering my first two 50-minute, repeat, back-to-back multiact, amateur volunteer talent shows in the middle of the plaza of a 55-story building that housed my corporation's headquarters in downtown Los Angeles. I seriously wondered if my career as a public relations executive was going to be ruined or enhanced by show business. Would the executives and workers from the building's tenants and my own company, many dressed in their navy blue, gray, and black suits with coordinated ties and accessories, be receptive to the happiness, joy, and beauties of human self-expression and talent soon to be displayed by so many businessmen and businesswomen right there in the middle of "the plaza" during everyone's lunch hour?

Would the high-strung, headstrong, temperamental performers (who were employees of my company during their professional lives) be able to control their intense emotions and feelings and prove "there's no people like show people?"

Would the chorus voices blend and create goose bumps on the arms and up the backs of the audience? Would the soloists remember their parts? Would anyone notice that the tenor, who did not yet have his black tuxedo, was wearing a self-dyed, blackish polyester suit?

Would the ballerina be able to go "on point" on a black, infected big toe right there on the slick, cracked floor of the portable stage? Would the smeared Coca Cola save the day and make the stage sticky enough so that she could get up and stay up on her toes for only a minute and a half?

Would the comedian keep his jokes clean?

Would the members of the chamber ensemble stifle their rage at being limited to just 6 minutes and go ahead and play their piece? Would the pianist flown in from the Bay Area for a solo performance be as good as his demo tape, especially of concern in that during the dress rehearsal he was kind enough to share with me that he could not read music?

Would the members of the rock-and-roll band listen to the show's producer and artistic director and turn down their amps so that the audience's ears would not "bleed" when the band played?

Would the sound man mix the sound well enough to compensate for the gaps and weaknesses in the performances? And would he muffle the squeaks in the speakers before the audience cringed?

Would the spotlight rented especially for the occasion not blind or confuse the performers?

Would the huge, massively heavy, 14-foot royal blue velvet rear curtain stay up where we had struggled to clip it on the rented support bars the night before?

Would the spinning mirror ball come down on cue?

Would the invited representatives of my company's senior management show up, and would they be proud of their talented employees, or would they wonder what in the world all of this had to do with finance and how much did it cost?

Would anyone come to see the show?

Tension? Stress? What do you think?!

The shows? They were fantastic! You should have seen the smiles on the faces of everyone in both audiences. I was so proud of the performers that I could have burst the buttons off my suit jacket. The volunteers had given their all, and the show was a smash hit. Gosh, show business was great!

And what was my first thought as soon as the event was over?

"I need a reward!"

For quite some time I had eyed a big, soft, beige teddy bear on the top shelf of the pharmacy in the building, but I did not buy it because I thought that would be silly. After all, I was a grown-up executive. I decided I did not care if getting the bear was not professional and businesslike. I wanted him no matter what. So I walked right up to the counter and said, "How much is that teddy bear?" The cashier said, "90 dollars." "Did you say 19 dollars?" I asked, hopefully. And he replied, "I said, 9-0 dollars." "Oh," I said.

After only a second's hesitation, I handed over my credit card. I wanted and deserved a reward and I needed it right then and there. After all, I had just survived a major special event—my first multiact showcase, and that bear had to be mine. Today that bear sits comfortably in my bedroom, reminding me to follow the advice I am now going to give you.

Each and every time you have been responsible for a successful special event, you will know how much was involved to enable that success, and you will know how hard you worked. You will also know very well that you want, need, and deserve a reward. Do not wait for anyone to give one to you. You might wait forever. Go immediately to find the equivalent of your bear and buy it right then and there.

When you know you have done a good job as the coordinator of a special event and when you know that many people have benefited from your efforts, there is no better way to celebrate that wonderful feeling of accomplishment than by rewarding yourself with something you really want!

I wish you the very best of luck in all of your special events, and may you experience many wonderful and exciting rewards!

101 Steps to a Successful Special Event

Special Event Checklist

Name of event: _____

Dates of event: _____

Overall event coordinator: _____

Senior administrators involved: _____

_____

Benefiting organization/cosponsor: _____

_____

Type of event: ❑ Administrative   ❑ Staff development
                  ❑ Community service ❑ Fund-raiser
                  ❑ Social   ❑ Other: _____

Step Number	✔	Task	Responsible	Due Date
1.		Event approved by senior administrators (SA)		
2.		Date(s) selected		
3.		Date(s) put on senior administrator's calendars		
4.		Staff/coordinator appointed		
5.		Outside consultants selected		
6.		Need for volunteers determined		
7.		VIP/SA event chair chosen		

Step Number	✓	Task	Responsible	Due Date
8.		VIP/SA event chair confirmed		
9.		Location selected		
10.		Location approved		
11.		Location reserved		
12.		Budget prepared		
13.		Budget approved		
14.		Reservation deposits paid		
15.		Checklist developed		
16.		Time line established		
17.		Planning meetings scheduled		
18.		Name of event selected		
19.		Theme of event selected		
20.		Color scheme selected		
21.		Agenda developed		
22.		Keynote speakers selected		
23.		Keynote speakers confirmed		
24.		Entertainment/celebrities selected		
25.		Entertainment/celebrities confirmed		
26.		Invitation list developed		
27.		Invitations written/designed		
28.		Invitations printed/received		
29.		Invitations mailed		
30.		RSVP receipt system developed		
31.		Public relations planned		
32.		Public relations arranged		
33.		Ads written		
34.		Ads placed		

Step Number	✓	Task	Responsible	Due Date
35.		Speakers/trainers selected		
36.		Speakers/trainers confirmed		
37.		Speeches written		
38.		Speeches approved		
39.		Hotel/facility accommodations planned		
40.		Hotel/facility accommodations reserved/confirmed		
41.		Food/beverages planned		
42.		Food/beverages ordered		
43.		Travel arrangements planned		
44.		Travel arrangements reserved/confirmed		
45.		Parking planned		
46.		Parking reserved/confirmed		
47.		Guest arrivals planned		
48.		Guest departures planned		
49.		Audiovisual needs planned		
50.		Audiovisual needs ordered		
51.		Communication/office equipment planned		
52.		Communication/office equipment ordered		
53.		Security needs planned		
54.		Security needs ordered		
55.		Promotional/gifts/awards items planned		
56.		Promotional/gifts/awards items ordered		

Step Number	✔	Task	Responsible	Due Date
57.		Promotional/gifts/awards items received		
58.		Programs written/designed		
59.		Programs printed/received		
60.		Participants' packages planned		
61.		Participants' packages prepared		
62.		Physical needs planned		
63.		Physical needs arranged		
64.		Physical needs set up		
65.		Tear down/removal/return of physical items		
66.		Room decorations, signs, centerpieces planned		
67.		Room decorations, signs, centerpieces ordered		
68.		Room decorations, signs, centerpieces received		
69.		Room decorations, signs, centerpieces set up		
70.		Room decorations, signs, centerpieces torn down/given away		
71.		VIPs' special needs planned		
72.		VIPs' special needs ordered/confirmed		
73.		VIPs' hosts assigned for D-Day (event)		
74.		Registration/welcome system planned		
75.		Crowd control/flow planned		
76.		Volunteer support recruited		

Step Number	✓	Task	Responsible	Due Date
77.		Volunteer support trained		
78.		Transportation of physical items to/from event planned		
79.		Storage/set-up system of physical items planned		
80.		Event evaluation form written		
81.		Event evaluation form printed		
82.		D-Day staff and volunteer assignments made		
83.		D-Day minutes taken		
84.		General thank yous planned		
85.		General thank yous executed		
86.		Volunteers thanked		
87.		Event coordinator thanked		
88.		Event planning committee thanked		
89.		Debriefing meeting held		
90.		Event evaluation form analysis conducted		
91.		Event evaluation report written		
92.		Event evaluation report distributed		
93.		Event minutes distributed		
94.		Event master file made		
95.		Next year's event calendared		
96.		Next year's location selected		
97.		Next year's site reservations made		
98.		Next year's site deposit paid		
99.		Next year's coordinator appointed		

Step Number	✓	Task	Responsible	Due Date
100.		Next year's planning committee appointed		
101.		This year's coordinator rewards self!		

Notes: _____
_____
_____
_____
_____
_____
_____

BE SURE TO PUT A COPY OF THE FINAL EVENT EVALUATION REPORT
AND THE MASTER COPY OF THIS COMPLETED CHECKLIST IN THE
MASTER EVENT FILE FOR FUTURE REFERENCE.

Publicity Approval Form

Instructions

Use one approval form for each separate publicity item. Attach a copy of the item for review. The completed form and item must be sent to the key school administrator responsible for the event, who will determine all other necessary approvals.

1. Check one: _____ Internal   _____ External
2. Describe the item to be approved: _____ Flier _____ News Release _____ Speech _____ Other: _____
3. Date of event: _____
4. Name of event: _____
5. Deadline for publication or release: _____
6. Name of person responsible for publicity:

   _____
7. Daytime phone: (_____) _____
8. Approvals: _____

	Signature	Date
1.		
2.		
3.		
4.		

APPENDIX C

Community Service Project Forms

Community Service Project Proposal Form

Instructions

The individual proposing this event provides the research to complete the information requested. The completed form is submitted to the appropriate faculty adviser or administrator for approval. PLEASE PRINT.

1. Event name: _____

2. Purpose of event: _____

3. Overall, inclusive dates of event: _____

4. Location(s): _____

5. Attach a budget request, if applicable.

6. Name of individual proposing event: _____

7. Daytime phone: (___) _____ FAX number: (___) _____

8. Name of organization to be served: _____

9. Mailing address: _____

10. City: _____ State: _____ Zip: _____

11. Phone: (___) _____ FAX number: (___) _____

12. Executive director/administrator: _____

13. Title: _____

14. Purpose of organization: _____

15. Does the organization have 501(c)3 status?   ❑ Yes   ❑ No

16. Contact at organization: _____

17. Title: _____

18. Daytime phone: (___) _____   FAX number: (___) _____

19. *Exact* volunteer involvement: _____

20. Number of volunteers needed: _____

Approvals

Name (Signature)	Title	Date
21.		
22.		
23.		
24.		
25.		

26. Additional comments: _____

_____

_____

_____

_____

_____

_____

_____

Community Service Project Planning Checklist

1. Event name: _____

2. Objective of event: _____

3. Date(s) of event: _____

4. Location(s) of event: _____

5. Phone number at event: Day (___) _____
   Evening (___) _____

6. Time(s) of event: _____

7. Name of project coordinator: _____

8. Daytime phone number of coordinator: (___) _____

9. Names/phone numbers of assistants:

Name	Phone Number
	(___) _____
	(___) _____
	(___) _____
	(___) _____
	(___) _____

10. VIPs attending and affiliation:

Name	Title	Affiliation

11. Benefiting organization(s): _____
_____
_____
_____

12. Key contacts/phone numbers at benefiting organization:

Name	Title	Phone Number
		(__) _____
		(__) _____
		(__) _____
		(__) _____
		(__) _____

13. Number of volunteers required: _____

14. Duties required of volunteers: _____

15. Number of volunteers/participants signed up: _____

16. Other important information: _____
_____
_____
_____
_____
_____
_____

Before Event

Target Date	Task	Person Assigned	Date Done	Notes
	Review event requirements			
	Get assistants			
	Create and send out fliers			
	Other publicity			
	Plan event			
	Complete budget			
	Make time line			
	Develop agenda			
	Complete sign-up form			
	Send confirmation to volunteers and participants			
	Supplies			
	Food/beverages			
	First aid			
	Photographer arranged			
	T-shirts ordered			
	Car pools			
	Name tags			
	Sign-in/sign-out supervisor			
	Emergency plan			
	Crowd control plan			

During Event

Target Date	Task	Person Assigned	Date Done	Notes
	Set up			
	Sign-in/sign-out all volunteers and participants			
	Name tags			
	T-shirts distribution			
	Supervise work			
	Tear down			
	Clean up			
	Thank you			

After Event

Target Date	Task	Person Assigned	Date Done	Notes
	Follow up			
	Thank yous sent			
	Debriefing			
	Evaluation form			
	Management report			
	Return all information and materials to appropriate administrator			

Community Service Project
Volunteer Sign-Up Form

Instructions

This form is completed and used by the project coordinator. One sign-up form is used for each separate date of the event. Attach all of the volunteer RSVP coupons or sign-up commitments to each *sign-up form* for reference throughout the planning of the event. PLEASE PRINT.

1. Event name: _____

2. Overall, inclusive dates of event: _____

3. Specific date of service: _____

Volunteer's Full Name	Homeroom Teacher	Guest (✓)	Guest of Whom?	Daytime Phone	Evening Phone
				( )	( )
				( )	( )
				( )	( )
				( )	( )
				( )	( )
				( )	( )
				( )	( )
				( )	( )
				( )	( )
				( )	( )
				( )	( )
				( )	( )
				( )	( )
				( )	( )
				( )	( )
				( )	( )

Community Service Project
Sign-In and Sign-Out Form

Instructions

The project coordinator must be sure to have each volunteer who participates in the event *sign in and sign out* so that credit will be given for all hours of service. PLEASE PRINT.

1. Event name: _____

2. Event date: _____

3. Project coordinator: _____

4. Daytime phone: (___) _____

Name (Please Print)	Guest (✓)	Guest of Whom?	Time In	Time Out	Total Time
EXAMPLE: Sue Smith			7:00 a.m.	6:00 p.m.	11 hrs.
EXAMPLE: Dave Smith	✓	Sue Smith	7:00 a.m.	6:00 p.m.	11 hrs.

Community Service Project
Summary Report Form

Instructions

The project coordinator completes this report. The *sign-in forms* that pertain to this report must be stapled to this form upon the completion of the project. Information used to complete this form comes from the *Community Service Project Proposal Form* and the *Sign-In and Sign-Out Forms*.

1. Report month/day/year: _____

2. Name of project coordinator: _____

3. Daytime phone: (___) _____

4. Project name: _____

5. Name of agency/school served: _____

6. Address: _____

7. City: _____ State: _____ Zip: _____

8. Overall, inclusive dates of service: _____

9. Total number of volunteers[*]: _____

10. Total hours of service: _____

11. Summary report completed by: _____

12. Daytime phone: (___) _____

*NOTE: A person can be listed and counted as many times as he or she volunteered on *separate* days.

APPENDIX D

Event Evaluation Form

Instructions

Immediately after the conclusion of the event, the lead event coordinator should complete this evaluation form and return it to the appropriate school administrator.

1. Event name: _____

2. Inclusive date(s) of event: _____

3. Agency(ies)/school(s) served if applicable: _____

4. Location(s) of event: _____

5. Please rate the success of the event:

1 ___ (*low*) 2 ___ 3 ___ 4 ___ 5 ___ 6 ___ 7 ___ 8 ___ 9 ___ 10 ___ (*high*)

6. Reasons for your evaluation:

_____

_____

_____

_____

7. Do you think the school should be involved in this event in the future?
   Yes _____ No _____ Why? _____

_____

_____

_____

8. Name of lead event coordinator: _____

9. Daytime phone: (_____) _____

10. Form completed by (if different from above): _____

_____

11. Daytime phone: (_____) _____

12. Date of completion: _____